KARM
RELATION

Esoteric Studies

Vol. V

RUDOLF STEINER

Seven lectures given in Prague and Paris
between 29th March and 25th May, 1924

Translated by D. S. Osmond

RUDOLF STEINER PRESS

Rudolf Steiner Press
Hillside House, The Square
Forest Row, RH18 5ES

www.rudolfsteinerpress.com

First edition 1966
Second edition 1984
Reprinted 1997, 2011, 2012

Originally published in German (with sixteen lectures) under the title
Esoterische Betrachtungen karmischer Zusammenhänge, Fünfter Band
(volume 239 in the *Rudolf Steiner Gesamtausgabe* or Collected Works) by
Rudolf Steiner Verlag, Dornach. This authorized translation published
by kind permission of the Rudolf Steiner Nachlassverwaltung, Dornach

Translation © Rudolf Steiner Press 1984

A catalogue record for this book is available from the British Library

ISBN 978 1 85584 257 1

Printed and bound by 4edge Ltd.

CONTENTS

karma may also *begin*. Speaking generally, qualities of soul in one life are transformed into bodily traits in another incarnation, and *vice versa*.   19

Prague, 30th March, 1924

3

Man's life in the physical body among the kingdoms of nature and after death among the Hierarchies of spiritual Beings. Pictures of the deeds of these Beings of the Hierarchies are revealed to man in his life after death and, when the time comes for the descent to incarnation, arouse in him the will to make compensatory adjustment for his dealings with individuals on Earth. Anthroposophy must speak not only to the head but awaken deep feeling in the heart when the spiritual world is described in detail. Studies of the practical working of karma must now be possible. The Mystery of Golgotha, Christianity and the effects of Mohammedanism. Influences of Arabism and the Crusades on European thinking. The Court of Haroun al Raschid and its cultivation of learning and the arts. Haroun al Raschid. Lord Bacon of Verulam. Amos Comenius. Ernst Haeckel. Pope Gregory VII (formerly Abbot Hildebrand). The fruits of each epoch of culture are carried onward to later times by human souls themselves. Realities in history.   35

Prague, 31st March, 1924

4

The nature and constitution of man can be understood only through a spiritual understanding of the Cosmos. Illustrations of how the deeds of one incarnation are carried over into a later one. Garibaldi and his bond with three contemporaries. Garibaldi, an Initiate of the ancient Hibernian Mysteries. Lord Byron. Rudolf Steiner's geometry teacher. The Palladium. Carl Marx. Muawiyah. Woodrow Wilson. Initiates of earlier epochs are hindered in their working by the bodies and education provided by the epoch during which they are incarnated. The 'twice-born'. The Sun Mystery and the early Christian Mysteries. The birth of Christ in the thirtieth year of the life of Jesus of Nazareth has been confounded with the physical birth. The sacrifice of intellect and the awakening of clairvoyant vision of Christianity as cosmic reality. Maurice Maeterlinck on Rudolf Steiner.   53

Prague, 5th April, 1924

5

Man in the life between death and rebirth. The aspects of 'death', the 'vanishing of earthly life', and the 'stars', revealed by Imagination, Inspiration, Intuition. The Moon-sphere and the primeval Teachers of mankind. The figure of Strader in the Mystery Plays. The soul passes into the Cosmos. The experience of earthly life in backward order as the first seed for the fulfilment of karma in the following incarnation.   69

Paris, 23rd May, 1924

6

After death man passes first into the region of the Elements, then into the region of cosmic Intelligence, then into the region of the Stars. Passage through the Moon-region, the Mercury-region, the Venus-region, the Sun-region, and the effects of existence in each of these spheres. Removal of the consequences of illness in the Mercury-sphere. Healing was the secret of the Mercury Mysteries. The Venus-region ruled by love. The Sun Mysteries and moral realities. Survey of seven-year periods in earthly life and the revelations of cosmic secrets.   79

Paris, 24th May, 1924

7

Mysteries of the Sun-existence: the province of the Exusiai, Dynamis and Kyriotetes. The Sun is the spiritual embryo of the future earthly life. The Christ was first in the Sun-sphere; since the Mystery of Golgotha He has been united with the Earth. After his sojourn in the Sun-sphere, man passes into the spheres of Mars-existence, Jupiter-existence, Saturn-existence. The elaboration of karma for the new earthly life through the divine deeds of the Seraphim, Cherubim and Thrones. Individual examples of karma elaborated in these spheres: Voltaire (Mars). Victor Hugo (Saturn). Eliphas Lévi (Jupiter).   91

Paris, 25th May, 1924

EDITOR'S PREFACE

During the year 1924, before his illness in September, Rudolf Steiner gave over eighty lectures, published with the title *Karmic Relationships: Esoteric Studies*, to members of the Anthroposophical Society in the following places: Dornach, Berne, Zürich, Stuttgart, Prague, Paris, Breslau, Arnhem, Torquay and London. English translations of these lectures are contained in the following volumes of the series:

Vols. I to IV. Lectures given in Dornach (49).
Vol. V. Lectures given in Prague (4) and Paris (3).
Vol. VI. Lectures given in Berne (2) Zürich (1), Stuttgart (3) Arnhem (3).
Vol. VII. Lectures given in Breslau (9).
Vol. VIII. Lectures given in Torquay (3) and London (3).

All these lectures were given to members of the Anthroposophical Society only and were intended to be material for study by those already familiar with the fundamental principles of Anthroposophy. The following extract from the lecture of 22nd June, 1924 (see Vol. II) calls attention to the need for exactitude when passing on such contents:

"The study of problems connected with karma is by no means easy and the discussion of anything that has to do with the subject entails—or ought at any rate to entail—a sense of deep responsibility. Such study is in truth a matter of penetrating into the most profound mysteries of existence, for within the sphere of karma and the course it takes lie those processes which are the basis of the other phenomena of world-existence, even of the phenomena of nature.... These difficult and weighty matters entail grave consideration of every word and every sentence spoken here, in order that *the limits within which the statements are made shall be absolutely clear...."*

7

The attention of readers is called to the fact that the fundamental explanations given by Rudolf Steiner of the laws and conditions of karma are contained in Vol. I of the series. Knowledge of the earlier lectures should therefore be regarded as an essential basis for study of those contained in the later volumes.

LECTURE 1

I want to begin these lectures for Members by speaking of how Anthroposophy lifts human consciousness above the earthly and material domain simply through the light it sheds upon the nature and being of man.

It is hardly possible for anyone immersed in modern civilisation to think otherwise than that during his life from birth to death he belongs to the Earth. Membership of a spiritual world is in most cases a mere belief or a dim inkling. Insight into the fact that man belongs to any world other than the Earth is scarcely within the power of human beings whose education and whole upbringing are the outcome of modern civilisation. Nevertheless, to believe that when man is being spoken of earthly conditions alone have to be considered is the great fallacy of all contemporary spiritual life in the West and in Middle Europe. The East alone has preserved a certain consciousness—although in a decadent form—of man's connection with the supersensible, cosmic powers and forces around the Earth. In olden times man felt himself dependent on the stars as well as on the plants and the animals around him on the Earth; he knew, too, that the Moon is not simply a physical orb revolving in space. Interest in the Moon to-day does not really go much further than attempts to discover whether there are or are not mountains or water there; hypotheses are advanced, but little thought is given to any other aspect of this neighbouring planet. As for the other heavenly bodies, investigation is entirely concerned with their physical conditions. In ancient times it was altogether different. Man was aware of his dependence on the heavenly bodies just as to-day he is aware of his dependence on the Earth.

9

I will start with something that has a certain scientific importance; it is an example that may perhaps not be to the liking of some people, but it is easy to follow. I have often emphasised in anthroposophical lectures that the formation of the human embryo in earthly life, even when investigated from the purely scientific point of view, provides the proof in itself that something *extra*-earthly is at work in the process. Natural science believes the ovum to be the most complex structure that can possibly exist on Earth. Much thought is given to this complex structure of the ovum and recently we have been hearing about the wonders of the atom and the molecule! The structure of a cell is said to be indescribably complex. But this is a fallacy, for the ovum is, in reality, *chaos;* it is not a complex structure. The chemical-physical structure goes to pieces, and before a living being can arise the ovum must have been in a state of chaos. The very purpose of fertilisation is to produce this state of chaos in the ovum, so that within the mother's organism there is matter which has been completely broken down. The processes in the mother's body produce this state of chaos. And now think of a crystal. The Cosmos cannot work in a crystal with its hard, firm edges; neither can the Cosmos work in the substance of a plant, which also has solid form; nor in that of an animal. Fertilisation means that the ovum becomes a chaos. Only then does the whole surrounding Cosmos work in upon this germinating entity and build up the living human form in such a way that the being of soul-and-spirit coming from earlier earthly lives can enter into it.

According to modern views this is so much nonsense—but it happens to be the truth! What is so deplorable in our time is that when one speaks the truth it is almost inevitably poohpoohed by contemporary scholarship. Some people may say: "This statement of yours may be based upon occult vision; but is it also capable of proof?" It is indeed—and in more ways than one might imagine. At our Institute for Biological Research in Stuttgart remarkable confirmation of this fact has come to light. Investigations have been made into the function of the spleen. You know, perhaps, that the

10

spleen has always been considered a very enigmatical organ. The story goes that in a viva voce examination the candidate was asked by the professor: "Can you tell me anything about the spleen?" The candidate puzzled his brains and at last blurted out in desperation: "I have forgotten it all." "What a pity!" said the professor. "Nobody has ever known anything about the spleen; you apparently were the only one, and you have forgotten it!"

I indicated a certain method, based on the principles of Spiritual Science, according to which Frau Dr. Kolisko has investigated the function of the spleen. The validity of her results is still being questioned but they will eventually win through, because the investigations were genuinely exact. During the investigations something else came to light. Because of the methods in general use to-day, one is sometimes obliged to adopt procedures that go much against the grain, but we finally decided to excise the spleens of rabbits. It was nothing in the least like vivisection but a quite simple operation; and we did everything that could possibly be done to avoid causing suffering. Unfortunately one of the rabbits died from a chill after the operation because by an oversight it was not taken immediately into the heated room. What result was to be expected from this operation? After the removal of the spleen something developed in the rabbit's body at the same place, something to which the Cosmos could have access. As long as the spleen itself was there the Cosmos could do nothing; but if the spleen is removed, the etheric spleen alone remains, and the etheric spleen adapts itself to the inworking forces of the Cosmos. It was to be expected, then, that at the place where the spleen had been, something would develop in the form that is a copy of the Cosmos, namely, the spherical form. And this is what we actually found! When we opened the rabbit we found a tiny organic body, spherical in shape; it had been produced by the inworking cosmic forces—when the condition in which the Earth alone works had been removed. This is entirely in line with the contention that the fertilised ovum is a body in which a state of chaos has been induced. And so karma led

11

us to an external proof of something that holds good in another sphere altogether.

In many respects it is the case that if a man's thoughts and feelings are the outcome of contemporary civilisation, his outlook is bound to be limited to the Earth; he is incapable of directing his gaze in any real sense to the Cosmos. Let me remind you of what is said in the book *Occult Science*, namely that the Moon and the Earth were originally one body, but that the Moon subsequently separated from the Earth. This fact is revealed to seership but it is also to some extent recognised by modern natural science. Particularly in the last few years a certain literary and scientific movement has been speaking—although in an erroneous way—of this relationship of the Moon to the Earth. The Moon in the heavens was once united with the Earth, was then ejected—if I may so express it—and since then has been circling around the Earth.

I must now speak of a second fact, connected with man's spiritual development in earthly existence. Even a purely external survey of what men have achieved on the Earth indicates the existence of a primordial, archetypal wisdom. It was not, of course, imparted in the abstract, intellectual forms demanded to-day, nor was it so closely bound up with the senses. It was imparted in a more pictorial, poetic form. Of this primordial wisdom itself, which existed on the Earth in times long before writing was known, nothing has remained. Echoes have been preserved in sagas and myths, in the wonderful Vedic literature, in the Vedanta and other Eastern texts. Anyone who steeps himself in this literature—not in the style of Deussen who sees only the outermost surface but for all that is an interpreter of great renown—anyone who can get to the depths of what this literature contains will have a profound reverence for the infinite wisdom there expressed in a pictorial, poetic form. He will feel that behind it all there was something unuttered and unwritten, perhaps even greater and more significant—a primordial, archetypal wisdom. How was this wisdom attained? Men did not study as we to-day, imbibing the contents of book after book and so gradually amassing a certain amount of information. Every human being who had developed a certain insight in those ancient times knew what Inspiration is, knew how to read in the world itself—not in books—when he induced in himself the right attitude of soul. He knew the reality of inner illumination; it was as real to him as the reading of books is real to us to-day. The priests in the Mysteries brought him to the stage where he was able to experience this inner illumination and become aware of spiritual reality in the Universe. This indeed was the purpose of the instruction he received in the Mysteries. He did not feel that the illumination came to him from the clouds. If we to-day were listening to someone talking from behind a screen, we should not attribute the voice to some undefined source but to an actual person. Similarly, a man who attained illumination knew: there are Beings on the Earth who, although they are not in physical incarnation, are the great Teachers of humanity. Man knew that he moved among Beings who were not, like himself, incarnate in flesh and blood but who were etheric Beings, imparting the illumination and the content of the primordial wisdom. He knew that the Earth was peopled not only by human beings of flesh and blood but by other Beings too, working and living in etheric bodies.

In studying these things we must get rid of the preconceived notion that humanity has lived on the Earth since the time of which records exist and that this was preceded by undefined conditions leading back to the man-ape or the ape-man. This is a really ludicrous idea! What the historians say holds good for a few centuries only, namely, that human beings have not changed fundamentally, except that they are supposed to have become cleverer. It is said that the Egyptians were a superstitious people, that they had mummies and other such customs, but apart from cleverness they are thought to have been just like modern men. Nothing is known with any certainty of the long period of previous history, but the view is that it leads back finally to the man-ape.

That is a view of evolution which must be abandoned! Man

13

peopled the Earth *before* the animals, only in a different form; man is the older being, as you can read in *Occult Science*. The ancient Teachers of the primeval wisdom did not incarnate in physical bodies but lived in spirit-bodies, and the men who communed with them, having experienced—as we ourselves experienced—the event of the separation of the Moon, knew that these Beings who had been among them as great Teachers had gone forth into the Cosmos, that they were no longer on the Earth but on the Moon. So that in truth not only the physical substance of the Moon but these spiritual Beings too, separated from the Earth. Once upon a time these Beings—who do not pass through birth and death in the same way as man—withdrew from the Earth and took up their abode on the Moon, although the actual substance of the Moon has been involved for long ages in a constant process of change.

This applies equally to man. In a period of seven to eight years the physical substances in the human body have completely changed. If anyone imagines that the bodies sitting here are the same as they were a few years ago, he is mistaken. The physical substance is entirely different; the soul-and-spirit has remained. Natural science is aware of this fact but pays no attention to it. The following question was once put to me after a lecture: "It is said that bees, as a hive, have a real link with the beekeeper, that if he has been very devoted to his bees and then dies, the hive is aware of his death and often dies too. How can this possibly happen? The bees as single entities have no faculties for knowing a human being, and the hive is only the sum total of the single bees!"—But this is by no means correct. I answered by using the following analogy. "Twenty years ago, two men were together. One of them goes to America, the other stays behind; after fifteen years the former returns from America and recognises his friend again. Yet not a single particle of the same physical substance has remained!"—And so it is not a question of each individual bee but of the intelligence of the beehive as a unit and that is not really so very different from human intelligence. As men, we are distinct from the cells

14

in our bodies, from our various organs. And just as no single particle of the bodies of those who attended my lectures ten years ago has remained, but only the soul-and-spirit, so, although the Moon-substance which once left the Earth has long since passed away, has been exchanged in the Cosmos, the *Beings* have remained. How these Beings have continued to participate in the life of earthly humanity is clearly revealed to the vision of Initiation, and to deeper observation of what we call *karma*. I will begin to speak about this to-day and continue in the following lectures.

When we make the acquaintance of a human being we do not as a rule give sufficient thought to the fact that we have really steered our whole earthly life towards this meeting. Acquaintance with another human being may take two forms. If we pay close attention we shall find more or less the following.—We get to know some person and feel aware of an intimate bond with him, no matter what he is like out-wardly—good-looking or ugly, intelligent or stupid. We pay no attention to his outer appearance; we feel an inner bond with him. That is the one alternative, in its extreme form. The other alternative is this.—We make the acquaintance of someone without feeling any inner bond, but he makes an intellectual or a moral impression upon us. We can describe him in great detail. Our relationship with the first acquain-tance is such that if, after our meeting, we are among other people who also know him, it goes against the grain to talk about him; we feel a kind of embarrassment; there is some-thing essentially *inward* in our relationship with him. But to talk about the second acquaintance is quite easy. We say that he is intelligent, or that he is a fool; we can describe the very shape of his nose, but we have no inner affinity with him. In the case of some people, no sooner have we made their acquaintance than we are always dreaming about them. We may get to know another person extremely well; we may be with him every day but we never by any chance dream about him because we have not been stirred inwardly. Very rarely indeed will there by anyone like *Garibaldi*, who felt the inner bond even before there was any direct, personal relationship.

15

Such cases are rare, but they do occur. The circumstances in which Garibaldi met his first wife are very interesting. External life affected him so little that he had no interest whatever in women. On a voyage to the coast of Brazil he happened to look at the land through his telescope and saw a girl standing on the shore. At that very moment he knew that she must become his wife. He hurried his ship to the land where a man greeted him in a friendly way and invited him to a meal at his house. Garibaldi accepted, and this man turned out to be the father of the girl he had seen through the telescope! Even before the meal was served he said to her—he spoke only Italian and she only Portuguese—that she must be his for life. She understood, and a very beautiful relationship was established between them. There you have a telling example of a karmic relationship. There was something heroic in the way the woman behaved. She accompanied Garibaldi on his campaigns in South America and when the news came that he had fallen on the battle-field, she went to search for him there. These were the circumstances in which she gave birth to her child, and in order to keep it warm she was obliged to strap it round her neck. Such experiences helped Garibaldi to find a firmer foothold in life. His wife eventually died and he married another woman whose acquaintance he made in an entirely conventional way; but this marriage lasted only for a day!

These are matters where karma stares us in the face, indicating two ways in which karma comes to expression between one human being and another. The karmic relationships differ entirely according to whether a man feels an inner bond or whether he can describe only the external characteristics of the other person.

When we study karmic experiences like that of an acquaintanceship where beauty or ugliness counts for nothing but where the feeling of kinship wells up entirely from within, we are led to discern the influence of those Beings of whom I have said that they were the original, primeval Teachers of mankind; they have remained active to this day, but now they work from outside, from the Cosmos. Such relationships

16

are of special interest to these Moon Beings and through them they participate in the most intimate way in the evolution of earthly humanity.

Just as there are Beings who belong to the Moon, so there are Beings who belong to the Sun. We have spoken of relationships where we find it easy to describe the other person in a more external way. In these cases it is the *Sun Beings* who interest themselves in the threads that are woven between soul and soul.

In studying human relationships we are led away from the Earth, first of all to the Sun and the Moon. There are human relationships in which we discern the working of the Moon; others in which we discern the working of the Sun. And so stage by stage we are led from the Earth to the Cosmos.

All that has been possible to-day is to make a beginning and we will continue in the lectures that are to follow.

LECTURE 2

In the lecture yesterday I gave certain indications in connection with the understanding of human destiny, and I said that an inkling of the power of destiny may come to a man from experiences which have had a significant effect upon his life. Suppose that at a certain age a man meets another human being; after the meeting their destinies run a similar course but the lives they both led hitherto have completely changed. An event like this meeting would have no rhyme or reason if it were entirely unconnected with previous happenings in their lives. Nor is this the case. Unprejudiced observation of the past reveals that practically every step taken in life was leading in the direction of this event. We may look right back into our childhood and we shall invariably find that some deed far removed in time from this event, that indeed the whole course of our life, led up to it as surely as if we had consciously and deliberately taken the path to it.

Such matters direct attention again and again to what in Anthroposophy we must call 'karmic relationships'.

I also said that acquaintanceships differ in character and as examples I quoted two extreme cases. We meet someone and form a bond with him, no matter what outward impression he makes upon our senses or aesthetic feelings. We do not think about his individual traits; our attraction to him is caused by something that wells up from within us. When we meet other human beings, we are not inwardly stirred in this way; we are more conscious of the appearance they present to our senses, our mental life, our aesthetic feelings. I said that this difference comes to expression even in the life of dream. We make acquaintanceships of the first kind and during the night, while we are living in the Ego and astral

19

body outside the physical and etheric bodies, we immediately begin to be aware of the persons in question; we dream about them. The dreams are a sign that something within us has been set astir by the meeting. We meet others of whom we do not dream because they have not stirred us inwardly and nothing wells up from within. We may be quite near to them in life but we never dream about them because nothing that reaches into our astral body and Ego-organisation has been set astir.

We heard that such happenings are related to the extra-earthly forces with which man is connected and of which modern thought takes no account—the forces working in upon the Earth from the surrounding, super-terrestrial Universe. We learned that the forces proceeding from the spiritual Moon Beings are connected with the whole of a man's *past*. For the past is in very truth working in us when immediately we meet a human being we are impelled towards him by something that wells up from within.

Speculation and dim feelings must, however, be replaced by Initiation-science which can actually bring to light the inner connections of these things. The Initiate before whom the spiritual world lies open, has both kinds of experiences, but in far greater intensity than is possible to ordinary consciousness. In the one case, where something rises up from within into the ordinary consciousness, a definite picture or a whole series of pictures filled with living reality rise up from within the Initiate when he meets the other human being and are there before him like a script he is able to read. The experience is quite clear to him; he himself is there within the picture which rises up in this way—it is as if an artist were painting a picture but instead of standing in front of the canvas were weaving in the canvas itself, living in every colour, experiencing the very essence of the colour. The Initiate knows that the picture arising in this way has something to do with the human being he meets. And through an experience resembling that of meeting a person again after the lapse of many years, he recognises in the human being standing physically before him, the replica of

20

the picture that has risen up in him. As he compares this inner picture with the man before him, he knows that it is the picture of experiences shared in common with him in earlier earthly lives. He looks back consciously into an earlier epoch when these experiences were shared between them. And as a result of what he has undergone in preparation for Initiation-science, he experiences in a living picture—not in dim feeling as in ordinary consciousness—what he and the man he now meets passed through together in a previous earthly life or a number of previous lives. Initiation-science enables us to see a picture of experiences shared with a man with whom we are karmically connected; it rises up with such intensity that it is as if he were to break away from his present identity and stand before us in his earlier form, coming to meet *himself* in the form he now bears. The impression is actually as vivid as that. And because the experience has such intense reality, we are able to relate it to its underlying forces and so to discover how and why this picture rose up from within us.

When man is descending to earthly life from the existence he spends in worlds of soul-and-spirit between death and a new birth, he passes through the different cosmic regions— the last being the Moon-sphere. As he passes through the Moon-sphere he encounters those Beings of whom I spoke yesterday, saying that they were once the primeval Teachers of humanity. He meets these Beings out yonder in the Universe, before he comes down to the Earth, and it is they who inscribe everything that has happened in life between one human being and another, into that delicate substance which, as opposed to earthly substances, the oriental sages have called 'Akasha'. It is really the case that whatever happens in life, whatever experiences come to men, every-thing is observed by those Beings who, as Spirit Beings not incarnate in the flesh, once peopled the Earth together with men. Everything is observed and inscribed into the Akasha substance as living reality, not in the form of an abstract script. These spiritual Moon Beings who were the great Teachers during the age of primeval cosmic wisdom, are the

21

recorders of the experiences of mankind. And when in his life between death and a new birth a man is once again drawing near the Earth in order to unite with the seed provided by the parents, he passes through the region where the Moon Beings have recorded what he had experienced on the Earth in earlier incarnations. Whereas these Moon Beings, when they were living on the Earth, brought men a wisdom relating especially to the past of the Universe, in their present cosmic existence they preserve the past. And as man descends to earthly existence, everything they have preserved is engraved into his astral body. It is so easy to say that man consists of an Ego-organisation, an astral body, an etheric body, and so forth. The Ego-organisation is most akin to the Earth; it comprises what we learn and experience in earthly existence; the more deeply-lying members of man's being are of a different character. Even the astral body is quite different; it is full of inscriptions, full of pictures. What is known simply as the 'unconscious' discloses a wealth of content when it is illumined by real knowledge. And Initiation makes it possible to penetrate into the astral body and to bring within the range of vision all that the Moon Beings have inscribed into it—as, for example, the experiences shared with other human beings. Initiation-science enables us to fathom the secret of how the whole past rests within man and how 'destiny' is shaped through the fact that in the Moon-existence there are Beings who preserve the *past* so that it lies within us when we again set foot upon the Earth.

And now another case. When the Initiate meets a man in connection with whom the ordinary consciousness simply receives an aesthetic or mental impression unaccompanied by dreams, no picture rises up in him, to begin with. In this case the gaze of the Initiate is directed to the Sun, not to the Moon. I have told you of the Beings who are connected with the Moon—in the same way, the Sun is not merely the gaseous body of which modern physicists speak. The physicists would be highly astonished if they were able to make an expedition to the region which they surmise to be full of incandescent gases and which they take to be the

Sun; at the place where they have conjectured the presence of incandescent gases, they would find a condition that is not even space, that is less than a void—a vacuum in cosmic space. What is space? Men do not really know—least of all the philosophers who give a great deal of thought to it. Just think: if there is a chair here and I walk towards it without noticing its presence, I hit against it—it is solid, impenetrable. If there is no chair I walk through space unhindered.

But there is a third possibility. I might go to the spot without being held up or knocked, but I might be sucked up and disappear: here there is no space, but the antithesis of space. And this antithesis of space is the condition in the Sun. The Sun is *negative* space. And just because of this, the Sun is the abode, the habitual abode, of the Beings who rank immediately above man: Angeloi, Archangeloi, Archai. In the case of which I am speaking, the gaze of the Initiate is directed towards these Beings in the Sun, the spiritual Beings of the Sun. In other words: a meeting of this kind that is not part of a karmic past, but is quite *new*, is for the Initiate a means of coming into connection with these Beings. And the presence is revealed of certain Beings with some of whom man has a close connection, whereas with others the connection is more remote. The way in which these Beings approach the Initiate reveals to him—not in detail but in broad outline—what kind of karma is about to take shape; in this case it is not old karma but karma that is coming to him for the first time. He perceives that these Beings who are connected with the Sun have to do with the *future*, just as the Moon Beings have to do with the past.

Even if a man is not an Initiate, his whole life of feeling will be deepened if he grasps what Initiation-science is able to draw in this way from the depths of spirit-existence. For these things are in themselves a source of enlightenment. A comparison I have often used is that just as a picture can be understood by a man who is not himself a painter, so these truths can be understood by one who is not himself an Initiate. But if a man allows these truths to work upon him, his whole relationship to the Universe is immeasurably

23

deepened. When man looks up to the Universe and its structure to-day, how abstract, how prosaic and barren are his conceptions! When he looks at the Earth he is still interested to a certain extent; he looks at the animals in the wood with a certain interest. If he is cultured, he takes pleasure in the slender gazelle, the nimble deer; if his tastes are less refined, these animals interest him as game; he can eat them. He is interested in the plants and vegetables, for all these things are directly related to his own life. But just as his feelings and emotions are stirred by his relationship with the earthly world, so his life of feeling can be stirred by the relationship he unfolds to the Cosmos beyond the Earth. And everything that comes over as destiny from the past— if it makes an impression upon us—impels us in heart and soul to look up to the Moon Beings, saying to ourselves: "Here on the Earth men have their habitations; on the Moon there are Beings who once were together with us on the Earth. They have chosen a different dwelling-place but we are still connected with them. They record our past; their deeds are living reality within us when the past works over into our earthly existence."

We look upwards with reverence and awe, knowing that the silvery moon is but the sign and token of these Beings who are so intimately connected with our own past. And through what we experience as men, we enter into relationship with these cosmic, super-earthly Powers whose images are the stars, just as through our carnal existence we are related with everything that lives on the Earth. Looking with expectation towards the future and living on into that future with our hopes and strivings, we no longer feel isolated within our own life of soul but united with what is radiating to us from the Sun. We know that the Angeloi, Archangeloi and Archai are Sun Beings who go with us from the present on into the future. When we look up into the Cosmos, perceiving how the radiance of the Moon is dependent upon the radiance of the Sun and how these heavenly bodies are interrelated, then out yonder in the Cosmos we behold a picture of what is living within our very selves. For just as

Sun and Moon are related to one another in the world of stars, so is our past—which has to do with the Moon—related to our future—which has to do with the Sun. Destiny is that in man which flows out of the past, through the present, on into the future. Woven into the Cosmos, into the courses of the stars and the mutual interplay of the stars, we behold the picture—now infinitely magnified—of what lives within our own being.

Our vision is thereby widened and penetrates deeply into the cosmic spheres. When a man passes through death he is released, to begin with, from his physical body only. He is living in his Ego-organisation, his astral body, his ether-body. But after a few days his ether-body has released itself from the astral body and from the 'I'. That which he now experiences is something that emerges as it were from himself; to begin with it is not large, but then it expands and expands—it is his ether-body. This ether-body expands into cosmic space, out into the very world of the stars—thus it appears to him. But as it expands the ether-body becomes so fine, is so rarefied, that after a few days it vanishes from him. But something else is connected with this. While our ether-body is being given over to the Cosmos, while it is expanding and becoming finer and more rarefied, it is as though we were reaching out to the secrets of the stars, penetrating into the secrets of the stars.

As we pass upwards through the Moon-sphere after death, the Moon Beings read from our astral body what we experienced in earthly existence. After our departure from earthly existence we are received by those Moon Beings, and our astral body in which we are now living is for them like a book in which they read. And they make an unerring record of what they read, in order that it may be inscribed into the new astral body when the time comes for us to descend to the Earth again.

We pass from the Moon-sphere through the Mercury-sphere, the Venus-sphere and then into the Sun-sphere. In the Sun-sphere, everything we have lived through, everything we have brought about and achieved in earlier incarnations becomes living reality within us. We enter into communion with the Beings of the higher Hierarchies, participating in their deeds, and we are now right within the Cosmos. Just as during earthly existence we move about on the Earth, are confined as it were within earthly conditions, we are now living in the cosmic expanse. We live in the infinite expanse, whereas on the Earth we lived in a state of confinement. As we pass through our existence between death and a new birth, it seems to us as though on the Earth we had been imprisoned . . . for everything has now widened into infinitudes. We experience the secrets of the Cosmos, but not as if they were in any way governed by laws of physical nature: these laws of nature seem to us then to be insignificant productions of the human mind. We experience what is happening in the stars as the deeds of the Divine-Spiritual Beings and we unite ourselves with these deeds: as far as in us lies we act among and together with these Beings. And from the Cosmos itself we prepare for our next earthly existence.

What we must realise in all its profound significance is that during his life in the Cosmos between death and a new birth, man himself fashions and shapes what he bears within him. In external life man perceives little, very little, of his own make-up and organisation. An organ can only really be understood when there is knowledge of its cosmic origin. Think of the noblest organ of all—the human *heart*. Scientists to-day dissect the embryo, observe how the heart gradually takes shape and give no further thought to the matter. But this outer, plastic structure, the human heart, is in truth the product of what each individual, in co-operation with the Gods, has elaborated between death and a new birth. In the life between death and a new birth man must work, to begin with, in the direction leading from the Earth towards the zodiacal constellation of Leo. This stream which flows from the Earth towards the constellation of Leo teems with forces and it is along this direction that the human being must work in order that when the time comes he may project the germinal beginnings of the heart—a vessel in which cosmic forces are contained. Then, having passed through this region in the far spaces of the Universe, man comes to regions nearer the Earth; he passes into the Sun-sphere. Here again forces are at work which bring the heart to a further stage of development. And then man enters the region where he is already in contact with what may be called the Earth-warmth. Out yonder in cosmic space there is no Earth-warmth, but something altogether different. In the region of the Earth-warmth the preparation of the human heart reaches the third stage. The forces streaming in the direction of Leo out of which the human heart is fashioned are purely moral and religious forces; in its initial stages of development the heart contains only moral and religious forces. To anyone who realises this it seems outrageous that modern natural science should regard the stars merely as neutral, physical masses, ignoring the moral element altogether. When man is passing through the Sun-region, these moral forces are taken hold of by the etheric forces. And it is not until man comes still nearer to the Earth, to the warmth, that the final stages of preparation are reached; it is then that the forces which shape the physical seed for the being of soul-and-spirit who is descending, begin to be active.

Each organ is produced and shaped by cosmic forces; it is a product of these cosmic forces. In very truth man bears the stars of heaven within him. He is connected with the forces of the whole Cosmos, not only with the plant-world through the substances which he takes into his stomach and which are then absorbed into his organism. These things can, of course, only be understood by those who have the gift of true observation. A time will come when the macroscopic aspect of things will be considered as well as the microscopic—which has really become a cult nowadays. People try to discover the secrets of the animal organism, of the human organism, by deliberately shutting off the Cosmos. They peer down a tube and call this microscopic investigation; they dissect a minute fragment, put it on a glass plate and try to eliminate the world and life as much as ever they possibly can. A tiny fragment is separated and studied by means of an instrument that cuts off any vista of the world surrounding it. There is, of course, no reason to belittle this kind of investigation for it brings wonderful things to light. But no real knowledge of man can be obtained in this way.

When we look from the Earth out into the Cosmos beyond the Earth, then, for the first time, part of the world is revealed. For after all it is only a part that becomes visibly manifest. The stars are not what they present to the physical eye—what the eye beholds is merely the sense-image—but to this extent they are, after all, visible. The whole world through which we pass between death and a new birth is invisible, supersensible. There are regions which lie above and beyond the world that is revealed to the senses. Man belongs to these realms of supersensible existence just as surely as he belongs to the world of sense. We can have no real knowledge of the being of man until we consider the life he has spent in the vast cosmic expanse. And then it dawns upon us that when, having passed through the gate of death into the Cosmos, we have returned to the Earth once again, the co-nections with this cosmic life are still alive within us. There is within us a being who once dwelt on the Earth, ascended into the Cosmos, passed through the cosmic realms and has again come down into a restricted existence on Earth. Gradually we learn to perceive what we were in an earlier existence on Earth; our gaze is carried away from the physical, transported into the spiritual. For when we look back into earlier earthly lives the power inherent in Initiation-science takes from us all desire for materialistic pictures.

In this connection, too, many strange things have happened. At one period there were certain theosophists who knew from oriental teachings that man passes through many earthly lives, but they wanted a materialistic picture although they deceived themselves to the contrary. It was said at that time that the physical organism of man disintegrates at death but that an atom remains and passes over in some miraculous way to the next earthly life. It was called the 'permanent atom'. This was simply a way of providing a materialistic picture. But all inclination for materialistic thinking of this

28

kind vanishes when one realises that in very truth the human heart is woven and shaped by the Cosmos.

The *liver*, on the other hand, forms in the near neighbourhood of the Earth; the liver has only little direct connection with the cosmic expanse. The knowledge gradually acquired from Initiation-science makes us realise that the heart could not exist at all if it had not been prepared and inwardly formed by the Cosmos. But an organ like the liver or the lung only begins to form in the neighbourhood of the Earth. Viewed from the Cosmos, man is akin to the Earth in respect of the lungs and liver; in respect of the heart he is a cosmic being. In man we begin to discern the whole Universe. According to spiritual anatomy, the lungs and certain other organs might be depicted by sketching the Earth; the forces contained in these organs operate in a realm near the Earth. But for the heart one would have to make a sketch of the whole Universe. The whole Universe is concentrated, compressed, in man. Man is in truth a microcosm, a stupendous mystery. But knowledge of the macrocosm into which man is transformed after death is free from every element of materiality. We now learn to recognise the true connections between the spiritual and the physical, between one quality of soul and another.

For example, there are people who have an innate understanding of their environment, of the human beings around them in the world. If we observe life we shall find individuals who come into contact with numbers and numbers of others, but they never really get to know them. What they say about these other people is invariably uninteresting and tells one nothing essential. Such individuals are incapable of really sinking into the being of others, they have no understanding of them. But there are other individuals who possess this gift of understanding. When they speak of another person their words are so graphic and explicit that one knows at once what the man is like without ever having met him; he is there before one. The description need not be detailed. A man who can sink himself in the being of another is able to convey a complete picture of him quite briefly. Nor need it necessarily be another individual; it may be something in nature. Many people try to describe a mountain, or a tree, but one despairs of getting any real picture; everything is empty and one feels parched. Other individuals again have the gift of immediate understanding; one could easily paint what they describe. Such a gift or defect—understanding of the world or obtuseness—has not come from the blue but is the result of an earlier earthly existence. If with Initiation-science one observes a man who has a deep understanding of his human and non-human environment, and then investigates his preceding earthly life—I shall have much to say on this subject—one discovers the particular qualities of his character in that earlier life and how they were transformed between death and a new birth into this understanding of the world around. And one finds that a man who understands the world around him was by nature capable of great *joy*, great happiness, in the preceding life. That is very interesting: men who in their previous life were incapable of feelings of joy are incapable, now, of understanding human beings or the world around them. A man who has such understanding was one who in an earlier life took delight in his environment. But this quality, too, was acquired in a still earlier life. How does a man come to have this joyousness, this gift of taking delight in his environment? He has it if in a still earlier earthly life he knew how to *love*. Love in one earthly life is transformed into joy, happiness; the joy of the next earthly life is transformed into warm understanding of the surrounding world in the third life.

In perceiving the sequence of earthly lives one also learns to understand what streams from the present into the future. Men who are capable of intense hatred carry over into the next earthly life as the result of this hatred the disposition to be hurt by everything that happens. If one studies a man who goes through life with a perpetual grudge because everything hurts him, makes him suffer, that is what one finds. Naturally one must have compassion for such a man but this trait in the character invariably leads back to a previous incarnation when he gave way to hatred. Please do not misunderstand me here. When hatred is mentioned it is natural for everyone to say: "I do not hate, I love everybody." But let them try to discover how much hidden hatred lurks in the soul! This becomes only too evident when one hears human beings talking about each other. Just think about it and you will realise that the derogatory things that are said about an individual far outweigh what is ever said in his praise. And if one were to go into the true statistics it would be found that there is a hundred times—really a hundred times—more hatred than love among human beings. This is a fact although it is not generally acknowledged; people always believe that their hatred is justified and excusable. But *hatred* is transformed in the next earthly life into hypersensitiveness to suffering and in the third life into lack of understanding, obtuseness—traits which make a man hard and indifferent, incapable of taking a real interest in anything.

Thus it is possible to survey three consecutive incarnations through which a law is operating: love is transformed into joy, joy is transformed in the third life into understanding of the environment. Hatred is transformed into hypersensitiveness to suffering and this again, in the third life, into obtuseness and lack of understanding of the world around. Such are the connections in the life of soul which lead over from one incarnation to another.

But now let us consider a different side of life. There are individuals—it is perhaps for this very reason that they are as they are—who have no interest at all in anything except themselves. Now whether a man takes real interest in something or takes no interest at all, has great significance in life. In this respect, too, odd things come to light. I have known men who had been talking to a lady in the morning but in the afternoon had not the slightest idea of what kind of hat or brooch she was wearing, or the colour of her clothes! There are people who simply do not observe such things. It is often regarded as a very excusable trait but in reality it is anything but that. It is really lack of interest, often going to such lengths that a man simply does not know if the person he met was wearing a black or a light coat. There was no inner connection with what stood before his very eyes. This is a somewhat radical example. I do not suggest that a man falls into the clutches of Ahriman or Lucifer when he does not know whether the lady he was talking to had fair or dark hair, but I merely want to indicate that individuals either have or have not a certain amount of interest in their environment. This is of great importance for the soul. If a man is interested in what is around him, the soul is invariably stimulated by it, lives with the environment. But whatever is experienced with lively interest, with real sympathy, is carried through the gate of death into the whole cosmic expanse. And just as man must have eyes in order to see colours on the Earth, so in his earthly existence he must be stimulated by interest, in order that it may be possible for him between death and a new birth to behold spiritually all that is experienced in the Cosmos. If a man goes through life without interest, if nothing captivates his eyes or his attention, then between death and a new birth he has no real connection with the Cosmos, he is as it were blind in soul, he cannot work with the cosmic forces. But when this is the case, the organism and the bodily organs for the next life are not being rightly prepared. When such a man enters the sphere of forces streaming in the direction of Leo, the rudimentary preparations for the heart cannot be made; he comes into the Sun-region and is unable to work at its further development; then, in the region of terrestrial warmth, the Earth-warmth, he is again unable to complete the preparation; finally he comes down to the Earth with a tendency to heart trouble.

Thus does *lack of interest*—which is an attribute of the life of soul—work over into the present earthly life. The nature of illness can only become fully clear when one is able to perceive these connections, when one perceives how the physical disability from which an individual is now suffering arose from something appertaining to the life of soul in a previous incarnation and has been transformed in the present incarnation into a physical characteristic. Physical sufferings in one incarnation are connected with experiences of a previous incarnation. Generally speaking, human beings who are said to be 'bursting with health', who never get ill, who are always robust and healthy, lead one's gaze back from their present existence to earlier lives when they took the deepest interest in everything around them, observed everything with keen and lively attention.

Naturally, things appertaining to the spiritual life must never be pressed too far. A stream of karma may also *begin*. Lack of interest may begin in the present life; and then the future will point back to it. It is not a question only of going back from the present to the past. Hence when karma is at work one can only say, *as a rule* it is the case that certain illnesses are connected with a particular trait or quality of soul.

Speaking generally, then, it may be said that qualities of soul in one earthly life are transformed into bodily traits in another earthly life; bodily traits in one earthly life are transformed into qualities of soul in another life. Now it is the case that anyone who wants to perceive karmic connections must often pay attention to what seem to be insignificant details. It is very important that the gaze should not be riveted on things that in the ordinary way are considered to be of outstanding significance. In order to recognise how one earthly life leads back to an earlier life, the gaze will frequently have to be directed to traits that seem of secondary importance. For example, I have tried—in all seriousness of course, not in the way that such investigations are often made—to discover the karmic relationships of various figures in history and in the sphere of learning, and my attention fell upon a personality whose inner life expressed itself so radically and remarkably that he ended by coining unusual forms of words. He has written a number of books in which the strangest forms of words occur. He was a very severe critic of social conditions, of men and their dealings with one another. He also deplored the jealousy shown by many learned men in their behaviour to their colleagues. He quotes examples to illustrate the tricks and intrigues of

33

certain scholars in an effort to down their fellows, and the chapter in question is headed: *Schlichologisches in der wissenschaftlichen Welt* (underhand ways in the scientific world). Now when a man coins an expression like *Schlichologisches*, one feels that it is characteristic. And an alert, inner perception of what lies behind such expressions leads to the discovery that in a previous incarnation this personality had to do with all kinds of warlike undertakings, often calling for a great deal of manoeuvring and camouflaged actions. This was transformed, karmically, into a flair for coining such expressions for intrigues, disputes, quarrels. In the word-pictures used for facts now under his observation, his head was describing that which in an earlier life he had carried out with feet and hands. And so in connection with this particular person I was able to give illustrations of how the physical had in a certain way been transformed into traits of soul.

LECTURE 3

Prague, 31st March, 1924

In the lecture yesterday I spoke of certain aspects of karma operating through the earthly lives of men, and of the forming of destiny, and I shall try to-day to give you an idea of how destiny actually takes shape.

When a man passes through the gate of death he comes into a spiritual world that is not, so to speak, more devoid of happenings and beings than our physical world, but infinitely richer. Understandable as it may be that it is never possible to do more than describe one phenomenon or another from the wide orbit of this spiritual world, the different descriptions given will have conveyed some idea of the infinite richness and manifoldness of man's life between death and a new birth. Here on the Earth, where our life between birth and death runs its course, we are surrounded by the several kingdoms of nature: by minerals, plants and animals, and by the physical human kingdom. Apart from the human kingdom, we rightly consider that the beings comprised in these other kingdoms belong to a rank below that of man. During his earthly existence, therefore, man feels himself—and rightly so—as the highest being within these kingdoms of nature. In the realm into which he enters after death, exactly the opposite is the case: man feels himself there to be the lowest among orders of Beings ranking above him. In anthroposophical literature I have, as you know, adopted for these Beings the names used in olden times to designate the higher Hierarchies. The first is the Hierarchy immediately above man, linked with him from above as the animal kingdom on Earth is linked with him from below. This is the Hierarchy of the Angeloi, Archangeloi and Archai. Then, above this Hierarchy, comes that

of the Exusiai, Dynamis, Kyriotetes, and then the highest
Hierarchy of all—the Thrones, Cherubim and Seraphim.
There are nine ranks, three times three ranks of Beings
higher than man. Between each group of three higher ranks
(ranging from below upwards) there is a parallelism with
the three lower stages (ranking from above downwards) of
animal, plant, mineral.—Only by including *all* these ranks
have we a complete picture of the world to which man
belongs.

Human existence may also be characterised by saying that
at physical birth or conception man passes from a purely
spiritual existence into the realm of the natural orders of
animal, plant, mineral; when he passes through the gate of
death he enters the realm of Beings ranking above him.
Between birth and death he lives in a physical body which
connects him with the kingdoms of nature; between death
and a new birth he lives in a 'spirit-body' which connects
him with the Beings of the higher Hierarchies. Here on
Earth our attention is directed, first and foremost, to our
environment; we feel on a level with this world and from the
Earth we look upwards to the Heavens, to the realm of
spirit—whatever may be the designation used in the different
religions. From the Earth man looks upwards with his
longings, with his piety, with his highest aspirations in
earthly existence. And in trying to envisage the spiritual
realm above him, he uses imagery borrowed from the earthly
world, he pictures what is above him in forms derived from
earthly existence. In the life between death and a new birth
it is the opposite: his gaze then is directed downwards from
above. You may say, "But this means that his gaze is
directed to an inferior world." That is not the case, for the
earthly world presents a quite different aspect when seen
from above. And precisely in the study of karma it will
become clear to us how different happenings on the Earth
appear when seen from above.

Having entered the spiritual world through the gate of
death, we come, first of all, into the realm of the lowest
Hierarchy: Angeloi, Archangeloi, Archai. We feel linked

with this next higher Hierarchy and we are aware that just as in the earthly realm everything around us means something to our senses, what the spiritual realm contains means something to the innermost core of our soul. We speak of minerals, of plants, of animals, inasmuch as we see them with our eyes and touch them with our hands, inasmuch as they are perceptible in a material sense. Between death and a new birth we speak of Angeloi, Archangeloi, Archai, inasmuch as these Beings have a connection with the innermost core of the soul. And passing on through the long existence spent between death and a new birth, we learn gradually to become part of the life of the Beings of the next higher Hierarchy who are concerned with us and with one another. These Beings are as it were the link connecting us with the spiritual outer world. During the first period of life between death and a new birth we are also very deeply occupied with ourselves, for the Third Hierarchy has to do with our own inner life and being. But then, after a certain time, our gaze widens: we come to know the spiritual world outside us, the objective spiritual world. Our leaders here are the Exusiai, the Dynamis, the Kyriotetes. They bring us into connection with the spiritual outer world. Just as here on Earth we speak of what is around us—mountains, rivers, forests, fields, whatever it may be—so do we speak in yonder world of that to which the Beings of the Second Hierarchy lead us. That is now our environment. But this environment is not a world of objects like the Earth; everything lives and has being, lives as spiritual reality. Nor in this life between death and a new birth do we come to know Beings only; we come to know their deeds as well, we feel that we ourselves are participating in these deeds.

But then a time comes when we feel how the Beings of the Third Hierarchy—Angeloi, Archangeloi, Archai—and the Beings of the Second Hierarchy—Exusiai, Dynamis, Kyriotetes—are working together with us at what we ourselves are to become in the next earthly life. A mighty, awe-inspiring vista opens before us. We behold the activities of the Angeloi, Archangeloi and Archai and we perceive how these

37

Beings act in relation to one another. Pictures come to us of what is proceeding among these Beings of the Third Hierarchy; but all these pictures are related to ourselves. And gazing at these pictures of the deeds of the Third Hierarchy, it dawns upon us that they represent the counter-part, the counter-image of the attitude of soul, of the inner quality of mind and heart that characterised us in the last earthly life. We now no longer say in terms of an abstract idea of conscience, "You were a man who acted unjustly to this person or that, whose thoughts were unjust." No, in the majestic pictures of the deeds of the Angeloi, Archangeloi and Archai, we behold the fruits of our attitude of mind and heart, of our life of soul, of our mode of thinking, in the last earthly life; we perceive images of this in what the Beings of the Third Hierarchy are doing. Our attitude, our feelings towards other individuals, towards other earthly things, are now outspread in the spiritual sphere of the Universe. And we become aware of what our thinking and our feeling signify. Here on the Earth this inner activity manifests in maya, as if it were enclosed within our skin. Not so in the life between death and a new birth. The manner of its appearance then is such that we know that whatever thoughts, feelings or sentiments we unfold are part of the whole world, work into and affect the whole world.

Echoing the East, many people speak of maya, of the illusion of the external world; but it remains an abstract thought. Studies like those we have been pursuing make us aware of the deep import of the words: "The world surrounding us is maya, the great illusion." We realise, too, what an illusory view prevails of the life of soul. We think that this is our affair and ours alone, for the truth is revealed only during our existence between death and a new birth. We perceive then that what seemed to be enclosed within us forms the content of a vast and majestic spiritual world. As our life after death continues, we observe how the Beings of the Second Hierarchy, the Exusiai, Dynamis and Kyriotetes, are connected with the faculties we have acquired in earthly life as the fruits of diligence, activity, interest in the things and happenings of the Earth. For having cast into mighty pictures our interest and diligence during the last earthly life, the Exusiai, Dynamis and Kyriotetes then proceed to shape images of the talents and faculties we shall possess in our next earthly life. In the images and pictures fashioned by the Beings of the Second Hierarchy we behold what talents and faculties will be ours in the next incarnation.

The course of this life continues and when the middle point of time between death and a new birth is about to be reached, something of particular importance takes place. From our habitations here on Earth—especially in those moments when as we look upwards to the firmament of heaven the stars send down their shimmering radiance—we feel the sublimity of the heavens above us. But something of far greater splendour is experienced as we gaze—downwards now—from the realms of spirit. For then we behold the deeds of the Beings of the First Hierarchy, of the Seraphim, Cherubim and Thrones working in mutual interrelationship. Mighty pictures of spiritual happenings are revealed to us as we gaze downwards—for our heaven now lies below. Just as in physical existence on Earth we gaze at the starry script above us, so when we look downwards from the realm of spirit we behold the deeds of the Seraphim, Cherubim and Thrones. And in this spiritual existence we are aware that what is proceeding among these Beings, revealed in sublime, majestic pictures, has something to do with what we ourselves are and shall become. For now we feel that what is taking place there among the Seraphim, Cherubim and Thrones reveals the consequences which our deeds of the previous earthly life will have in the earthly life to come. We perceive how in earthly life we behaved in this way to one individual, in that way to another individual, how we were compassionate or pitiless, whether our deeds were good or evil. Our attitude and disposition are the concern of the Third Hierarchy, our deeds of the First Hierarchy, the Seraphim, Cherubim and Thrones. Then, in the cosmic memory now alive in us, there arises a shattering, awe-inspiring realisation of our deeds and actions between birth and death in the last earthly life. Down below we behold the deeds of spiritual Beings, of Seraphim, Cherubim, Thrones. What are they doing? They show us, in pictures, what our experiences with individuals with whom we had some relationship in the previous incarnation will have to become in the new relationship that will be established in order that mutual compensation may be made for what happened between us in the previous life. And from the way in which the Seraphim, Cherubim and Thrones work in co-operation, we realise that the great problem is there being solved. When I have dealings with an individual in some earthly life, I myself prepare the compensatory adjustment; the work performed by the Seraphim, Cherubim and Thrones merely ensures that the compensation will be made, that it will become reality. And it is these Beings who also ensure that the other individual with whom I shall again make contact is led to me in the same way as I am led to him. It is the majestic experiences arising from the pictures of the deeds of the higher Hierarchies which are recorded by the Moon Beings and subsequently inscribed by them in our astral body when the time comes for the descent to another earthly existence. Together with us in the life between death and a new birth, these Moon Beings witness what is happening in order that the adjustment of the previous earthly life may take place in a subsequent life.

This, my dear friends, will give you an inkling of the majesty and grandeur of what is here revealed, as compared with the sense-world. But you will realise, too, that the things of the sense-world conceal far, far more than they actually make manifest.

Having lived through the region of the Seraphim, Cherubim and Thrones, man passes to still other realms of existence. More and more the longing arises in him for a new incarnation in which compensation can be made for what he did and experienced in his previous earthly life.

Anthroposophy has failed in its purpose when it remains a mere collection of ideas and conceptions, when people speak abstractly of the existence of karma, of the way in which one incarnation works over into another. Anthroposophy is only fulfilling its real purpose when it speaks not only to the head but awakens in the heart a feeling, a discernment, of the impressions that can be received in the supersensible world through the Beings of that world. It seems to me that nobody with an unprejudiced, receptive mind can listen to such communications about the supersensible world as I am now giving, without being inwardly stirred. We ought to be able to realise that although here on Earth we live through the whole gamut of human experiences, from deepest suffering to supreme happiness, what we are able to experience of the spiritual world should affect us far more potently than the most intense suffering or the highest happiness. We can only have the right relationship to the spiritual world when we admit, "In comparison with earthly sufferings or earthly happiness, what we are able to experience of the truths and beings of the spiritual world remains shadowy"—as indeed it does to those who merely listen to information about Initiation-science. But to Initiates themselves it is far from shadowy. We should also be able to say, "I can feel how deeply what is here imparted about the spiritual world would affect the soul, if the soul had only sufficient strength and energy." A man should ascribe it to earthly weakness if he is incapable of experiencing every degree of feeling, from fiery enthusiasm to deepest suffering, when he hears about the spiritual world and the Beings of that world. If he ascribes to his own weakness the fact that he is unable to feel these things with due intensity, then the soul has gone some way towards establishing the true and right relationship to the spirtual world.

When all is said and done, what value is there in spiritual knowledge if it cannot penetrate to the concrete facts or indicate what is really taking place in the spiritual world! We do not expect our fellow-men on Earth to talk about a meadow in the way that pantheists or monists or would-be philosophers talk about the Godhead; we expect a detailed description of the meadow. And the same applies to the spiritual world. It must be possible to describe the concrete details. People to-day are still unaccustomed to this. Many who are not out-and-out materialists will accept generalities about the existence of a spiritual world and so forth. But when this spiritual world is described in detail they often become indignant because they will not admit that it is possible to speak in this way of the Beings and happenings of the spiritual world. If human civilisation is not to fall into chaos, more and more will have to be said about the realities of the spiritual world. For earthly happenings too remain obscure when people have no understanding of what lies behind them.

In this connection, my dear friends, there is something in the destiny of the Anthroposophical Society that strikes a note of tragedy. But if the necessary understanding for these things becomes more widespread, at any rate among Anthroposophists themselves, there is justification for hoping that good may develop out of the tragedy, that from the Anthroposophical Society there may go forth a quickening of the civilisation that is so obviously heading for the chaos of materialism. But if that quickening is to be a reality, something must be understood which at the beginning was not understood—which can more easily be understood to-day because more than two decades of effort have passed since the founding of anthroposophical work.

At the beginning, as you know, the Anthroposophical Movement was within the Theosophical Movement. When we founded in Berlin the Section from which the Anthroposophical Society eventually developed, I wanted at our first gathering to strike a kind of keynote for what ought really to have followed. And now that we have tried through the Christmas Meeting at the Goetheanum to re-organise the Anthroposophical Society, I am able to speak about a certain fact to which probably very little attention has been paid hitherto. Nor could it have been otherwise here, because as far as is known to me none of our friends from Bohemia was present at the time. I gave a first lecture which was similar in character to the lectures given later on to the Groups. This first lecture had an unusual title, one which might at the time have been considered rather daring. The title was: "Studies of the practical working of karma." (*Praktische Karmaübungen.*) My intention was to speak quite openly about the way in which karma works.

Now the leading lights of the Theosophical Movement who at that time regarded me as something of an intruder, were present at the meeting and they were convinced at the outset that I was not qualified to speak of inner, spiritual matters. At that period the leading lights of the old Theosophical Movement were always reiterating: "Science must be upheld, account must be taken of modern science. . . ." Well and good—but nothing much came of it. Things have now been set on the right path but only the very first steps have been taken; nor will anything essential have been achieved until we have advanced beyond these first steps. And so what was intended in those early days all became rather theoretical. "Studies of the practical working of karma" were announced but nobody at that time would have understood their import, least of all the leading lights of the Theosophical Society. It therefore remained a task which had to be pursued under the surface as it were of the anthroposophical stream, performed as an obligation to the spiritual world. But to-day—and how often it has been so during the development of the Anthroposophical Movement—I am reminded of the title of what was to have been the first anthroposophical Group lecture: "Studies of the practical working of karma." I can also remember how shocked the leading lights of the Theosophical Society were by such a presumptuous title.

But time marches on and more than two decades have elapsed since then—much has been prepared, but this preparatory work must also have its results. And so to-day these results must become reality. "Studies of the practical working of karma" which one desired—rather boldly—to begin at that time, must be actually undertaken. Such indeed was the aim of our Christmas Meeting: to bring real and living esotericism into the Anthroposophical Movement. This must be taken in all earnestness. By formalism alone the Anthroposophical Movement will have no regenerating

43

effect upon our civilisation. In the future we must not shrink from speaking quite openly about the things of the spiritual world.

I want to begin to-day to speak of spiritual realities underlying earthly happenings and the life of humanity on Earth. Within the whole process of earthly evolution stands the Mystery of Golgotha—the Event which imbued this evolution with meaning. To deeper observation, everything that preceded this Event was in the nature of preparation. And although on account of the shortcomings of men and the influence of the Luciferic and Ahrimanic Powers from the spiritual side, the impediments to progress are more in evidence than the progress itself, it is nevertheless true that *since* the Mystery of Golgotha everything proceeding from the physical and spiritual worlds alike has come to pass for the sake of bringing man further along the path of world-evolution as a whole. The gifts of Christianity to humanity will—if men prove worthy to receive them in their deeper, spiritual significance—be revealed only in times to come. But the essential impulse—and this applies, as well, to everything that Anthroposophy can achieve—lies in the Mystery of Golgotha.

We know that the influence of the Mystery of Golgotha made its way, to begin with, across the South of Europe and on into Middle Europe. But I do not want to speak of that to-day. I want you to think of how Christianity spread across the North of Africa into European civilisation. You know that some six hundred years after the founding of Christianity through the Mystery of Golgotha, a different religious stream —the stream of Mohammedanism—spread across from Asia. In contrast to Christianity, the spiritual life that is connected with the name of Mohammed expresses itself more in abstractions. In Christianity there are many more direct descriptions of the spiritual world than there are in Mohammedanism. But it has been the destiny of Mohammedanism to absorb much ancient science, much ancient culture. We see how Mohammedanism comes over from Asia and spreads in the wake of Christianity. It is an interesting spectacle. We see the stream of Christianity flowing towards the North, reaching Middle Europe; we see, too, how Mohammedanism twines as it were around this Christian stream—across North Africa, Spain and on into France.

Now it is quite easy to realise that had Christianity alone been at work, European culture would have taken a quite different form. In an outer, political sense it is of course true that Europe repulsed the waves of Mohammedanism—or better said, of Arabism. But anyone who observes the spiritual life of Europe will realise, for example, that our modern way of thinking—the materialistic spirit on the one side and science with its clear-cut, arabesque-like logic on the other—would not have developed had Arabism not worked on, despite its setbacks. From Spain, from France, from Sicily, from North Africa, mighty and potent influences have had their effect upon European thinking, have moulded it into forms it would not have assumed had Christianity alone been at work. In our modern science there is verily more Arabism than Christianity!

Later on, as a result of the Crusades, much Eastern culture —by then, of course, in the throes of decadence—came directly to the ken of the European peoples. Many of the secrets of Eastern culture found their way to Europe through this channel. In Western civilisation, above the stratum of Christianity, lie those elements of oriental spiritual life which were absorbed into Arabism. But you see, none of this is really understandable when perceived only from the outside; it must all be perceived from within. And from within, the spectacle presented to us is that although wars and victories brought about the suppression of Arabism and the bearers of Mohammedanism, the Moors and so forth, nevertheless the souls of these people were born again and continued to work. Nothing whatever can be gained from abstract accounts of how Arabism made its way to Europe from Spain; insight can only arise from a knowledge of the inner, concrete facts.

We will consider one such fact. At the time of Charles the Great in European history—it was at the end of the 8th and

45

beginning of the 9th centuries—*Haroun al Raschid* was living over in Asia, in Bagdad, in an entourage of brilliant oriental scholarship. Everything then existing in the way of Western Asiatic learning, indeed of Asiatic learning in general, had been brought together at the Court of Haroun al Raschid. True, it was all steeped in Mohammedanism, but everything in the way of culture—mathematics, philosophy, architecture, commerce, industry, geography, medicine, astronomy—was fostered at this Court by the most enlightened men in Asia. People to-day have little conception of the grandeur and magnificence of what was achieved at the Court of Haroun al Raschid. First and foremost there was Haroun al Raschid himself—not by any means a ruler of mediocre intelligence or one who merely for the sake of self-glorification called to his Court the greatest sages of Western Asia, but a personality who in spite of unwavering adherence to Mohammedanism was open and receptive to everything that oriental civilisation had to offer. At the time when Charles the Great was struggling with difficulty to master the rudiments of reading and writing, much brilliant learning flourished at the Court of Bagdad. The conditions in which Charles the Great lived are not comparable in any way with those brought into being by Haroun al Raschid.

This was at a time when many regions of Western Asia and wide territories in Africa had already adopted Mohammedanism, and the brilliant learning cultivated at the Court of Haroun al Raschid had spread far and wide. But among the wise men at that Court—men deeply versed in geography, in nature-lore, in medicine and so forth—was many a one who in still earlier incarnations had belonged to ancient Mystery Schools. For men who were Initiates in an earlier life do not always give direct evidence of this in another incarnation. In spite of having been an Initiate in earlier Mysteries, it is only possible for a man in any given epoch to absorb the spirituality and develop the constitution of soul which the body of that particular epoch allows. Seen in its essential nature, the life of the soul does not tally with the intellectual ideas of the psyche in man prevailing at the present time. The soul lies at a far deeper level than is usually imagined.

Let me give you an example. Think of a personality like *Ernst Haeckel*. The first impression one gets of him is that his view of the world is coloured by materialism, that he expounds a kind of mechanism by which the life of nature and also the life of soul is determined, that in his invectives against Catholicism he is sometimes fascinating, sometimes fanatic, and sometimes, too, lacking in taste. One who is cognisant of the threads connecting the different earthly lives of a human being will pay little attention to these traits; he will look at the deeper qualities of soul. Nobody who in trying to observe the actual manifestations of karma allows himself to be blinded by Haeckel's most striking external characteristics will be able to discover his previous incarnation. In order to find Haeckel's previous incarnation attention must be paid to the way and manner in which he expounded his views. The fact that Haeckel's erudition bore the stamp of materialism is due to the age in which he lived; that, however, is unimportant; what *is* important is the inner constitution and attitude of soul. If this is perceived by occult sight, then in the case of Haeckel the gaze is led back to *Pope Gregory VII*, the former Abbot Hildebrand—actually one of the most impassioned advocates of Catholicism. If one compares the two personages, knowing that both come into the picture here, one will perceive that they are the same and also learn to recognise the unessentials and the essentials in respect of the great affairs of humanity as a whole. The theoretical ideas themselves are by no means the prime essential; they are only essential in this abstract, materialistic age of ours. Behind the scenes of world-history it is the quality, the *modus operandi*, of the soul that is all-important. And when this is grasped it will certainly be possible to perceive the similarity between Gregory VII and his reincarnation as Haeckel.

Insight of this kind has to be acquired in studying the concrete realities of karma, and if it is to mean anything to us to be told that at the Court of Haroun al Raschid, for example, there were men who, although their physical bodies and education make them appear outwardly to be typical products of the 8th and 9th centuries, were nevertheless the reincarnations of Initiates in ancient Mysteries. When the eye of spirit is directed to this Court, a certain personality stands out in bold relief—one who was a deeply discerning, influential counsellor of Haroun al Raschid, and for that epoch a man of great universality. A remarkable destiny lay behind him. In a much earlier incarnation, and in the same region afterwards ruled over by Haroun al Raschid, but inhabited, then, by quite different peoples, he had participated in all the Initiations which had there taken place, and in a later incarnation, as a different personality, he had striven for Initiation with deep and intense longing, but was unable to achieve it because at that time destiny prevented it. Such a personality lived at the Court of Haroun al Raschid but was for this reason obliged to conceal deep down in his inner life what lay within him as the fruits of the earlier incarnation as an Initiate. The inability to achieve Initiation occurred in a later incarnation and after that came the incarnation at the Court of Haroun al Raschid. And at this Court, for the reason that in those times Initiations in the old sense were no longer possible—this personality was one who out of a strong inner impulse and with powerful and sound imagination, organised and vitalised everything that was cultivated at this Court. Scholars, artists, a whole host of poets, representatives of all the sciences, were to be found there; moreover Bagdad itself at that time was the centre of the very widespread scientific and artistic activity prevailing in the empire of the Caliphs. The organisation of it all was the work of this personality—a personality endowed with great powers of initiative. Such individuals invariably play a significant rôle in the onward march of civilisation.

Let us think of Haroun al Raschid himself. If with occult sight one discerns the qualities of soul he possessed and then tries to discover whether he has since reincarnated, one finds that Haroun al Raschid continued to be associated with and to carry further what he had instituted on Earth; having passed through the gate of death he participated, spiritually, in the earthly evolution of mankind; from the spiritual world his influence was considerable but he himself assimilated a great deal. And then, in the form appropriate to the epoch, this personality came again as *Lord Bacon of Verulam*, the founder of modern science. From England, Bacon of Verulam gave a strong impetus to European thinking. You may say: but what a different personality from Haroun al Raschid! . . . Nevertheless it is the same individuality. The outward differences are a matter of the external world only. We see the soul of Haroun al Raschid after death moving across from Asia and then, from the West, influencing the later civilisation of Europe, doing much to lay the foundations of modern materialism.

The other personality—he who had been not only the right hand but the very soul of Haroun al Raschid's Court and had had that strange spiritual destiny—this personality took a different path. Far from seeking a life of outward brilliance, the urge in this soul after death was to unfold a rich inner life, a life of deep inwardness. Because this was so, there could be no question of taking a path leading to the West. Think again of Haroun al Raschid and his Court— outward brilliance and magnificence, inner consolidation of the fruits of civilisation, but at the same time the impulse to externalise everything contained in Mohammedanism. This was bound to come to expression in a subsequent incarnation. The wide and all-embracing application of scientific method had to come to the fore—and so indeed it did. The outward brilliance that had characterised the Court of Haroun al Raschid came to clear expression in Bacon himself.

The other personality who had been the very soul of the Court in Bagdad was of a deeply inward nature, closely related to what had been cultivated in the ancient Mysteries. This could not come to expression—not at any rate until our own time when, since Kali Yuga is over and the Michael Age has begun, it is possible once again to speak openly of the spiritual. Nevertheless it was found possible to pour what had been received from the Mysteries in such volume and

49

with such vital power into civilisation that its influence was profound. Something of the kind may be said in connection with the other personality whose development in the spiritual world after death was such that finally, when the time arrived for a new incarnation, he could not land, so to speak, in the Western world where materialism had its rise; he was led, inevitably, to Middle Europe and was able there to give expression to the impulse deriving from the ancient Mysteries but conforming with the altered conditions of the times. This personality lived as *Amos Comenius*. And so in the later course of world-history these two souls who had lived together at the Court of Bagdad took different paths: the one as it were circling the South of Europe in order, from the West, as Bacon of Verulam, to become the organising genius in modern literature, philosophy and the sciences; the other taking the overland path—as did the Crusades—towards Middle Europe. He too was a great and gifted organiser but the effects of what he achieved were of an entirely different character. It is a wonderful and deeply impressive spectacle— there they were, Amos Comenius and Bacon of Verulam, having taken different paths. The fact that the period of their lives did not exactly coincide is connected with world-karma, but ultimately—if I may express it in a trivial way— they met in Middle Europe. And a great deal that is needed in civilisation would become reality if the esoteric influences contained in the work of Amos Comenius were to unite with the power achieved by the technical sciences founded through Bacon of Verulam. This outcome of the paths taken by two souls who in the 8th and 9th centuries worked at the Court of Haroun al Raschid is one of the most wonderful illustrations of how world-history runs its course. Haroun al Raschid makes his way across Africa and Southern Europe to England, whence his influence works over into Middle Europe; Amos Comenius takes the path which brings him to Middle Europe, and in what develops from his achievements there he meets the other soul.

Only when history is studied in this way does it become reality. What passes over from one epoch of world-history into another does not consist of abstract concepts; it is human souls themselves who carry onward the fruits of each epoch. We can only understand how what makes its appearance in a later epoch has come over from an earlier one, when we perceive how the souls themselves develop onwards from one epoch to the next. The distinction between what is called 'maya' and inner reality must everywhere be taken earnestly. Perceived in its outward aspect only, history is itself maya; it can only be rightly understood by getting away from the maya and penetrating to the truth.

We will continue these studies in the next lecture to Members. May the right kind of understanding be forthcoming as we now pursue the task inaugurated by the Christmas Foundation Meeting: to make into a reality what was announced at the very beginning, perhaps rather naively, as 'Studies of the practical working of karma'. After preparation that has been going on for decades now, a genuine study of karma and of its manifestations will certainly be possible in the Anthroposophical Society without causing misunderstanding and apprehension.

LECTURE 4

Prague, 5th April, 1924

Previous studies in the Anthroposophical Society here in Prague will have made it clear to you that the evolution of mankind is governed by the spirit—or perhaps it is better to say, by spiritual Beings—and that human souls, themselves filled with spirit, carry over their achievements from one epoch to another, including, of course, whatever burden of guilt they have accumulated in a particular epoch. All these things enable us to gaze deeply into the life of the Cosmos both from the physical aspect and from the aspect of soul and spirit, and only in this way is it possible for us to understand our real nature and being. For without yielding to pride we must acknowledge that in our own human nature we are united with the spiritual fount of the Cosmos and that we can understand our own being and constitution only through a spiritual understanding of the Cosmos.

Now since the Christmas Foundation Meeting it is not only a matter of conducting the affairs of Anthroposophy within the Anthroposophical Society; the conduct of these affairs must in itself *be* Anthroposophy. And this must also come to expression in the re-casting of anthroposophical work. In these lectures, therefore, I have not been afraid to lead our study from exoteric into more esoteric domains, and in this respect I want to add something to-day to what has already been said—something that provides concrete evidence of how the human soul passes over from one epoch into another. The general principle applies equally to individuals, and through an understanding of the karma of personalities known to us all, light can be shed upon our own karma. To-day, therefore, we will continue our study of karma in more concrete detail.

In the course of these lectures I have mentioned the name of an individual who is a remarkable example of how a certain visionary quality can reveal itself in one who is pre-eminently a man of will. I have mentioned the name of *Garibaldi*, the hero of the cause of freedom in Italy, and I have also spoken of certain of his outstanding characteristics. Everything about him gives expression to will, to impulses of will. What a tremendous power of will was in evidence when as a young man during the twenties and early thirties of the 19th century he set out again and again, quite voluntarily, on perilous voyages through the Adriatic, and after having been taken prisoner several times was always able, through his strength and courage, to escape. What a tremendous power of will was at work when, having seen that for the time being there was no field for his activity in Europe, he went over to South America where he became one of the most intrepid fighters in the cause of freedom there. I have spoken, too, of how in the circumstances of his betrothal and marriage he disregarded the usual customs and determined his own life as he saw fit. Then, on his return to Europe, he became the one to whom, in reality, modern Italy owes everything.

When the question was put to me one day: "What could have been the karmic connections of this personality?" two aspects came into consideration. For the finding of karmic connections is by no means a simple but a very complicated task. I have said already that one must often start from details which although clearly in evidence seem to be of minor importance and be led by them to the principles according to which the facts of the one earthly life are carried over into the later life.

The case of Garibaldi is strange in that although at heart and in sentiment he was a republican, through and through a republican, he laid the whole force of his will into the task of consolidating the Italian monarchy under *Victor Emanuel*. Simply by studying the biography of Garibaldi one can perceive a fundamental contradiction between this inner trend of feeling and his actual deeds. One perceives, too, that he felt a bond with men like *Mazzini* and *Cavour*, with whose ideas and convictions he was manifestly at variance and whose trend of thought differed so radically from his own. Then there is the striking fact that Garibaldi was born, in the year 1807, quite near to the birthplaces of the other three: the later King Victor Emanuel, Cavour the statesman, and Mazzini the philosopher. Their birthplaces were really in close proximity. And then one is led to investigate the connection between the karma of such personalities.

The other aspect—a very far-reaching one—is the following. In studying Spiritual Science we must always have in our minds that in olden times there were Initiates, seers, men of vision in the widest sense. And the question may be asked: Since these wise men of times gone by must reincarnate, where are they working now, in the modern age? Where are they, these great personalities who worked as Initiates in the past?—They have indeed come again but it must be remembered that when a human being is born in a particular epoch he is obliged to use the body provided by that epoch. The bodies of olden days were more pliant, more flexible, yielding more readily to the spirit; and in earthly existence man must use the body to transform into earthly shape and earthly activity what was imbued into him before he came down to the Earth. Faced with conditions that are so full of riddles, we must remember—and no criticism is here implied—that for centuries now the effect of the whole of education upon the human organism has been such that what was once alive in an Initiate simply cannot come to expression. Much has to remain concealed in the deep substrata of existence. And for this reason, many Initiates of bygone days appear again as personalities who with the concepts and notions prevailing to-day cannot be recognised as former Initiates because they are obliged to use the body which their epoch provides.

Garibaldi is just such an example. If we go far back into the past, we find deep and profound Mysteries, great Initiates, in ancient Ireland. But the Irish Mysteries survived right on into the Christian era. Even to-day there is still much living spirituality in Ireland—not of an abstract, conceptual kind, but alive, spiritually potent. Chaotic as conditions in that country appear to-day, there is in Ireland much real spiritual life. But it is only the very last vestige of what once existed. In Hibernia, in Ireland, there were deep and penetrating Mysteries whose influences still made their way across to Europe in the early centuries of the spread of Christianity. And there one finds an Initiate whose path in the 8th to 9th centuries after the founding of Christianity led him from Ireland to the region corresponding approximately to modern Alsace. Under the stormy conditions then prevailing, this Initiate achieved much for the cause of true Christianity, for which, if the truth be told, Boniface accomplished very little. To this Initiate came three pupils from different quarters of the world—three pupils who entrusted themselves to him. These three pupils came to him—one from far away, another from nearer at hand. But in the Irish Mysteries there was an inviolable decree that an Initiate to whom pupils had entrusted themselves must not abandon them in the later incarnation but must accomplish in earthly life something that will hold them to him, something that establishes a bond between him and these pupils. The Initiate of whom I am speaking was born again as Joseph Garibaldi, with that visionary quality of will which in olden times had been able to express itself in a quite different form from that possible in a body belonging to the 19th century. Garibaldi received only a very inferior education, quite unlike the education that was typical of the 19th century. The three others I have named were the pupils who in the past had come to him from different parts of the world. But the impulse working from the one incarnation over into the other was far deeper and more potent than external principles of action. In comparison with the link stretching across the incarnations between man and man, it is a triviality to contend: I am a Republican, you are a Monarchist. In these things one must realise how greatly earthly maya, the great illusion, the semblance of being, deviates from the spiritual reality which is in truth the motive power behind the phenomena of existence. And so in spite of the radical difference in sentiment and conviction, Garibaldi could not abandon, for example,

Victor Emanuel. Sentiment and conviction in connection with earthly matters and not with human beings belong to the epoch, not to the individuality who passes from one earthly life to another.

I want to give another example, one with which I came into close personal contact. I had a *geometry teacher* who was of enormous help to me. My autobiography will have indicated to you that geometry is one of the subjects to which I owe most because of the impulses it quickened in me. This geometry teacher himself played a very valuable part in my life. The fact that he was an excellent constructor might well have led to my great affection for him because I myself loved geometrical construction and because he expressed everything with genuine independence of mind and also with all the exclusiveness belonging to geometrical thinking. His mind was focused so exclusively upon geometry that in the real sense of the word he was no mathematician; he was a geometrician and nothing else. In this sphere he was brilliant but it could not be said that he was deeply versed in mathematics. He lived at a time when all descriptive geometry— his special subject—underwent changes. Characteristically, however, he kept to the old forms. But something else about him provided a far more revealing clue for occult investigation: he had what is called a club-foot. Now the strange thing is that the force—not, of course, the physical substance —the force which a man has in his feet in one incarnation, the character of his tread, how his feet lead him into wrong-doing or well-doing—this force is metamorphosed. Whatever is connected with the feet may live itself out in a subsequent incarnation in the head-organisation; whereas what we now bear in our head may come to expression, in the later incarnation, in the organisation of the legs. Metamorphosis takes a peculiar form here. One who is conversant with these things can discern from the style and manner of a man's gait, how he treads with his toes and heels, what quality of thinking characterised him in an earlier incarnation. And one who observes the qualities of a man's thinking—whether his thoughts are quick, fleeting, cursory, or deliberate and

57

cautious—will be able to picture how he actually walked in a previous incarnation.

In the earlier incarnation, a man whose thoughts are fleeting and cursory walked with short, rapid steps, as though tapping over the ground, whereas the gait of a man who thinks cautiously and with deliberation was firm and steady in the earlier life. It is just these apparently minor characteristics that lead further when one is looking for the deeper, spiritual connections and not those of an external, abstract kind. And so when time and time again I called up the picture of this greatly loved teacher, I was guided to his earlier incarnation. With this picture another associated itself—also of a man with a club-foot: *Lord Byron.* The two men were there before me in this inner picture. And the karma of my teacher, as well as the peculiarity of which I have told you, led me to the discovery that in the 10th or 11th century, both these souls had lived in their earlier incarnations far over in the East of Europe where they came one day under the influence of a legend, a prophecy. This legend was to the effect that the Palladium, which in a certain magical way helped to sustain the power of Rome, had been brought to that city from ancient Troy, and hidden. When the Emperor Constantine conceived the wish to carry Roman culture to Constantinople he caused the Palladium to be transported with the greatest pomp and pageantry to Constantinople and hidden under a pillar, the details of which gave expression to his overweening pride. For he ordered an ancient statue of Apollo to be set at the top of this pillar, but altered in such a way as to be a portrait of himself. He caused wood to be brought from the Cross on which Christ had been crucified and shaped into a kind of crown which was then placed on the head of this statue. It was the occasion for indulging in veritable orgies of pride!

The legend went on to prophesy that the Palladium would be transferred from Constantinople to the North and that the power embodied in it would be vested eventually in a Slavonic Empire. This prophecy came to the knowledge of the two men of whom I have been speaking and they resolved

58

to go to Constantinople and to carry off the Palladium to Russia. They did not succeed. But in one of them especially —in Byron—the urge remained, and was then transformed in the later life into the impulse to espouse the cause of freedom in Greece. This impulse led Byron, in the 19th century, to the very region, broadly speaking, where he had searched for the Palladium in an earlier incarnation.

It is a question, you see, of finding the threads which lead back into earlier ages. On another occasion my attention fell on a personality who lived about the 9th century in the north-east of France as France is to-day, and who during the first part of his life was the owner of extensive landed estates. He was, for those times, a wealthy man, and being of a war-like nature he engaged in many rather quixotic military adventures—not on a large but on a small scale. When he had reached a certain age, this personality gathered around him people who then accompanied him on a campaign which ended in disaster and brought bitter disillusionment in its train. Without having achieved anything at all, he was obliged to return home. But meanwhile—as was a common practice in those days—another had taken possession of his house, land and people during his absence. On his arrival he found that his own estates were in other hands—strange as the story is, it actually happened so—and he was obliged thereafter to serve in his own manor as a kind of helot or serf. Many a meeting took place there with people of the neighbourhood, usually by night, and in a rather uncultured, rough-and-ready way, ideas were elaborated for seizing power—although beyond the fact that such ideas were worked out, nothing could possibly come of them. These ideas for rebelling against the overlords—almost as in the days of Rome—were the subject of much heated and fervid dialectic. Our interest may well be roused by this personality who had been ousted from estates, possessions and authority but who with an inflexible will stirred up the whole district, particularly against the one who had usurped the property. The personality of whom I am speaking was born again in the 19th century, when inwardly, in mind and soul, he

59

became the kind of character one would expect from the circumstances of the earlier incarnation: he became *Carl Marx* the socialist leader. Just think what a light is shed upon world-history when one can study it in this way, when one can actually follow the souls passing from one epoch into the other, observing how what these souls bear within them is carried over from epoch to epoch. History and the evolution of mankind are seen in this way in their real and concrete setting.

In Dornach recently I was able to call attention to another connection of karma, one which caused me repeatedly during the War, and especially at the end of the War, to warn people against allowing themselves to be blinded by a certain outstanding figure of modern times. In the Helsingfors lectures of 1913 I had already spoken of the very limited abilities of the person in question. This was because the connection between Muawiyah, a follower of Mohammed in the 7th century, and *Woodrow Wilson*, was clear to me. All the fatalism which characterised the personality of Muawiyah came out in the otherwise inexplicable fatalism of Woodrow Wilson—in his case, fatalism of will. And if anyone wants to find corroboration, to discover the origin of the well-known Fourteen Points, he has only to turn to the Koran. Such are the connections. These things must be kept absolutely free from sympathy or antipathy; it is not a question of criticism but only of the purest objectivity. But this very objectivity leads from one point in history at which a soul has appeared, to another such point. When humanity outsteps in some degree the still surviving heritage of materialism, people will be willing to listen to such things and observe for themselves. And then they will feel quite differently about their place in modern civilisation because they will be able to see it not in a dead but in a living setting. That is the important point. The whole process of historical development will be imbued with life. And if man is to get beyond the blind alley in which he is now standing in his civilisation, he needs the *living* spirit and not the dead spirit of abstract concepts and ideas.

In their study of history, people will probably be very reluctant to approach the spiritual in the way indicated in my public lecture here a few days ago, but nevertheless they will ultimately be obliged to do so. For ordinary historical study which has only documentary evidence to go upon is full of insoluble enigmas. Things of which the origins cannot be explained are forever cropping up. Why is it so? It is because the origins are not understood, they have been completely obscured. When such things are investigated, a great deal in history becomes living reality. But it also becomes apparent that men themselves have done a great deal to garble and falsify history in important respects.

It will certainly seem strange and perplexing when in connection with a relatively near past, the spiritual investigator is forced to assert that a wonderful work of art has been wiped out of existence by the hostility of a certain stream of spiritual life. In the early centuries of Christendom there was extant in the more southerly regions of European civilisation a literary work of art setting forth the nature of advancing culture immediately after Christianity had taken root in the evolution of humanity in Europe. This work of art—it was an epic drama, a dramatic epos—narrated how since the recent revelation of Christianity man cannot draw near to the true Being of Christ unless he undergoes a definite preparation similar to that given in the Mysteries.

In order to understand the real import of this, the following must be clear to us. To His intimate disciples Christ had made it abundantly clear that He, as a Sun Being, a Cosmic Being, had come down into the one born in the East as Jesus, in the thirtieth year of his life. Jesus of Nazareth was born into a Moon religion. What was the nature of the Jahve-, the Jehovah-religion, and of the Being Jahve himself? In looking upwards to Jahve, men were gazing, in reality, at the human 'I', the 'I' that is directly dependent upon the physical human configuration that is born with us. But what is born with us, what has taken shape and developed inasmuch as in the mother's body we were moulded into a vessel for the human 'I'—this is dependent upon the Moon forces. Jahve

61

is a Moon God. And in lifting their eyes to Jahve, men said to themselves: Jahve is the Regent of the Moon Beings, from whom proceed those forces which bear man into his physical existence on Earth.—But if Moon forces alone were at work, man would never be able to transcend what is laid into him in the life that belongs to the Earth. This he can no longer do of himself, but in earlier times it was different. If we go back into prehistoric ages we find something very remarkable, something that to the modern mind sounds extremely strange. We find that in the thirtieth year of life, human beings experienced a complete transformation of soul. This was the case in the great majority of people belonging to a certain class. Strange as it sounds to modern ears, it was really the case in an age of which the Vedas are mere echoes. There were men in ancient India to whom the following might happen.— When another man whom they had seen a few years previously came up to them, he might find that although they saw him, they did not recognise who he was; they had forgotten everything that had happened to them during the previous thirty years, they had forgotten it all—even their own identity. And there was an actual institution—we should call it, as we call every such institution to-day, an official department or board of authorities—to which such a person must apply in order to be informed who he was and where he had been born. Only when, in the Mysteries, these people had been given the necessary training were they able to remember their lives up to the age of thirty. They were men who at a later time, were called the 'twice born', who owed the first period of their existence to the Moon forces, the second to the forces of the Sun.

The metamorphosis which in ancient times came about in so radical a way in the course of earthly life, the 'being born a second time', was ascribed to the Sun—and rightly so, for the Sun forces have to do with what a human being is able, by dint of his own free will, to make of himself. But as the evolution of humanity progressed, this gradually ceased to be part of the process of development; man no longer brought down into the physical realm any consciousness of having gazed into the cosmic worlds. Julian the Apostate wished to revive the knowledge of these things and had to pay for the attempt with his death. But through the power enshrined in His words, Christ wished to bring to men through morality, through a deepening of the moral and religious life, what nature does not bring. It was Christ Who taught: "When you learn to feel as I feel, when instead of turning your eyes to the Sun you behold what is alive in me—who was the very last to receive the Sun-Word in the thirtieth year—then you will find the way to the essence of the Sun once again!" The teachers in the Mysteries during the early period of Christianity knew with certainty that the development of the intellect, of intellectuality, was then beginning; intellectuality does indeed bring man freedom but deprives him of the ancient clairvoyance which leads him into the *cosmic* spirituality. Therefore these wise men of the old Christian Mysteries instituted teaching which was then set forth in that epic drama of which I spoke. It was the narration of the experiences of a pupil in the Christian Mysteries, who by the sacrifice of intellect at a certain point in his youth was to be led to true Christianity when the realisation had dawned in him that Christ is a Sun Being Who came to dwell in Jesus of Nazareth from his thirtieth year onwards.

This epic was a moving and impressive narration of how a human being seeking the inmost truth of Christianity makes the sacrifice of intellect in early years—that is to say, he vows to the higher Spiritual Powers that intellectuality shall not be his mainstay but that he will so deepen his inner life that he may come to know Christianity not as mere history or tradition but in its cosmic reality and setting, seeing in Christ the Bearer of the spirituality of the Sun. A scene of dramatic grandeur and impressive content was presented by this transformation in a human being by the sacrifice of intellectuality. A human being who, to begin with, received Christianity merely according to the letter of the Gospels— as was customary later on—became one who learned to behold the cosmic realities and Christ's living connection with the Cosmos. The awakening of clairvoyant vision of

Christianity as cosmic reality—such was the content of that ancient epic drama. The Catholic Church took care to ensure that every trace of this epic should be exterminated. Nothing has remained—the Catholic Church has had power enough for that. It is only by accident that a transcript has been preserved of which, too, nothing would be known, had it not been from the hand of a personage living at the Court of Charles the Bald—from the hand of Scotus Erigena.

Those who realise the import of these things will not think it so strange when spiritual investigation urges one to speak of this epic story of a man who by vowing to sacrifice intellectuality was transformed in such a way that the heavens were opened to him. But in the form of tradition many a fragment from that ancient epic has survived, in substance largely unchanged, but no longer understood—above all its great setting and its imagery were no longer understood. The content of this work of poetic art became the subject of numerous paintings. These paintings too were exterminated and only traditions survived. Fragments of these traditions were known in a circle to which Brunetto Latini, the teacher of Dante, belonged. From this teacher Dante heard something of the traditions—not of course in precision of detail, but in aftermath—and in his Divine Comedy echoes from that old epic still live on. But the work existed, as truly and as surely as the Divine Comedy itself exists.

Recorded history, you see, does not tally with the realities and a great deal of what was exterminated by enemies will have to be discovered again through spiritual investigation. For it was all to the interests of a certain side to root out every indication that Christ comes from the Cosmos. The birth of Christ which actually took place in Jesus' thirtieth year has been confounded with the physical birth. What then became a Christian doctrine could never have been established had the epic drama of which I have spoken not been exterminated. The time will come when spiritual investigation will have to play a part if human civilisation is to make real progress.

You know the devastating effect of illnesses of the kind

64

which befell someone I once knew well. He held a post of considerable authority but one day he left his home and family, went to the railway station and took a ticket for a far distant place, having suddenly forgotten everything about his life hitherto—his intellect was in order but his memory was completely clouded. When he arrived at his first destination he took another ticket, travelling in this way through Germany, Austria, Hungary, Galicia, and finally, when his memory came back to him, he found himself in an asylum for the homeless in Berlin.

It is in truth the ruin of the whole Ego when a man forgets what he has lived through and experienced. It would also mean the ruin of the Ego of civilisation, the Ego of European humanity, were men to forget completely the things that were part of their historical experience, those things which have been rooted out. Spiritual Science alone can bring back the power of remembrance.

But even to men who, comparatively speaking, are kindly disposed, Spiritual Science still seems strange and foreign. One cannot read without a certain irony what a man, who is in other respects so promising, says about me as the founder of Anthroposophy. In *The Great Secret*, Maurice Maeterlinck seems unable to deny that the introductions to my books contain much that is reasonable. He is struck by this. But then he finds things which leave him in a state of bewilderment and of which he can make absolutely nothing.—We might vary slightly one of Lichtenberg's remarks, by saying: "When books and an individual come into collision and there is a hollow sound, this need not be the fault of the books!" But just think of it—Maurice Maeterlinck is certainly a high light in our modern culture and yet he writes the following—I quote almost word for word: 'In the introductions to his books, in the first chapters, Steiner invariably shows himself possessed of a thoughtful, logical and cultured mind, and then, in the later chapters he seems to have gone crazy' (See note, p109). What are we to deduce from this? First chapter—thoughtful, logical, cultured; last chapter—crazy. Then another book comes out. Again, to begin with, thoughtful, logical, cultured; and finally—crazy!' And so it goes on. As I have written quite a number of books I must be pretty expert at this sort of thing! According to Maurice Maeterlinck a kind of juggling must go on in my books. But the idea that this happens voluntarily . . . such a case has yet to be found in the lunatic asylums!

The books of writers who think one crazy are really more bewildering still. The very irony with which one is bound to accept many things to-day shows how difficult it still is for men of the present age to understand genuine spiritual investigation. Nevertheless such investigation will have to come. And in order that we shall not have been found wanting in the strength to bring about this deepening of the spiritual life, the Christmas Foundation Meeting was held as a beacon for the further development of the Anthroposophical Society in the direction I have indicated. The Christmas Foundation Meeting was intended, first and foremost, to inaugurate in the Anthroposophical Movement an epoch when concrete facts of the spiritual life are fearlessly set forth—as has been the case to-day and in the preceding lectures. For if the spirit needed by mankind is to find entrance, a stronger impetus is required than that which has prevailed hitherto.

It has been for me a source of real gladness that in the lectures here, given either to the public or to a smaller circle, the opportunity has been afforded me to lead a little further into the depths of spiritual life. And with this inner gladness let me express my heartfelt thanks for the cordial words addressed to me by Professor Hauffen at the beginning of this evening's session. I thank you for your welcome and for the way in which your souls have responded during my presence here. And you may rest assured that Professor Hauffen's words will remain with me as a wellspring of the thoughts which I shall constantly send you and which will be with you alike when you achieve your aims and when you are working here. Even when we are separated from one another in space we are, as Anthroposophists, together in our hearts, and this should be known and remembered. For many years

66

I have been privileged to speak in Prague of different aspects of the spiritual life and it has always been a source of satisfaction to me. Particularly is it so on this occasion, because the demands made upon your hearts and souls have been relatively new, because this time you have had to receive with an even greater open-mindedness what I had to say to you in discharging a spiritual commission. When I say 'spiritual commission', let us take these words to imply that in the spirit we remain together. The aim before us will be achieved if friends work together with all their hearts, if, above all, they remain united in anthroposophical thinking, feeling and willing.

Together with my thanks, please take this as a cordial farewell—betokening no separation but rather the establishment of a spiritual communion. This feeling of communion should flow through every word that is spoken among us. Everything that is said among us should serve to unite us more and more closely. In this sense let me assure you with all my heart that my thoughts will be with you, seeking to find among you one of those places where true anthroposophical will and the anthroposophical stream of spiritual life are able to work. And so we will go our ways, but in the body only, remaining spiritually and in our hearts together.

LECTURE 5*

Paris, 23rd May, 1924

In these three lectures I want to speak of how Anthroposophy can live as knowledge of the spiritual in the world and in man—knowledge that is able to kindle inner forces and impulses in the moral and religious life of soul. Because this will always be possible, Anthroposophy can bring to mankind something altogether different from anything produced by the civilisation of the last few centuries. This civilisation has actually suffered from the diffusion of brilliant forms of knowledge: natural science, economics, philosophy. But all this knowledge is a concern of the head alone, whereas moral-religious impulses must spring from the heart. True, these impulses have existed as ideals; but whether these ideals and the feelings associated with them are also powerful enough to create worlds of the future when the present physical world has passed away, is a question unanswerable by modern science. What has sprung from modern science is the widespread doubt that is characteristic of the present age and the age just past.

To begin with I want to consider three aspects of man's life. We ourselves, our destiny, are inextricably connected with this life from birth to death. Birth, or rather conception, is the boundary in one direction; death is the boundary in the other. Birth and death are not life; they are merely the beginning and the end of physical life. And the question is this: Can birth and death in themselves be approached with

---

* Before beginning this lecture, Dr. Steiner spoke words of greeting to the audience—which consisted of Members of the Anthroposophical Society only—and referred briefly to the importance and consequences of the Christmas Foundation Meeting held at Dornach in December, 1923. The text of his address will be found on pages 106/7.

69

the same mental attitude with which we contemplate our own life, or the life of others, between birth and death, or must our approach to the actual boundaries of birth and death be from a different vantage-point? Therefore the *aspect of death,* which so significantly sets a boundary to human life, shall be the first object of our study to-day.

At the end of a man's earthly life he is divested by death of the physical body we see before us. The Earth takes possession of it, either through its own elements as in burial, or through fire as in cremation. What can the Earth do with the part of man we perceive with physical senses? The Earth can do no other than subject it to destruction. Think of the forces in nature around us. They build up nothing when the human corpse is given over to them; they simply destroy it. The nature-forces around us are not there for the purpose of upbuilding, for the human body disintegrates when it passes into their grasp. Hence there must be something different which builds up the human body, something different from earthly forces, for they bring about its disintegration.

If, however, human death is studied with forces of cognition activated in the soul through the appropriate exercises, everything presents a different aspect. With ordinary faculties of cognition we see the corpse and nothing else. But when, by means of these exercises, we develop Imagination—the first stage of higher knowledge described in my books—then death is completely transformed. In death man tears himself from the grasp of the Earth; and if we cultivate Imagination, we see in direct vision, in living pictures, that in death man rises from his corpse—he does not die. At the stage of Imaginative Knowledge, physical death is transformed into spiritual birth. Before death, man stands there as earthly man. He can say: "I am here, at this place; the world is outside me."—But the moment death occurs the man himself is not where his corpse lies. He is beginning his existence in the wide spaces of the Universe; he is becoming one with the world at which he has hitherto only gazed. The world outside his body now becomes his field of experience and therewith what hitherto was inner world becomes outer world, what hitherto was outer world

70

becomes inner world. We pass out of our personal existence into world-existence. The Earth—so it appears to Imaginative cognition—makes it possible for us to undergo death. The Earth is revealed to Imaginative cognition as the bearer of death in the Universe. Nowhere except on Earth is death to be found in any sphere frequented by man, whether in physical or spiritual life. For the moment man passes through death and becomes one with the Universe, the second aspect presents itself—the aspect in which the widths of space appear to be everywhere filled with cosmic thoughts. For Imaginative vision and for the man himself who has passed through death, the whole Cosmos now teems with cosmic thoughts, living and weaving in the expanse of space. The space-aspect becomes the great revealer. Having passed through death man enters a world of cosmic thoughts; everything works and weaves in cosmic thoughts. This is the *second aspect*.

When we confront a man in earthly life, he is there before us in the first place as a personality. He must *speak* if we are to know his thoughts. So we say: "The thoughts are within him; they are conveyed to us through his speech." But nowhere within the perimeter of earthly life do we discover thoughts which stand alone. They are present only in men, and they come out of men. When we pass from the earthly sphere of death to the space-sphere of thoughts, to begin with we encounter no beings in the widths of space—neither gods nor men—but everywhere we encounter cosmic thoughts. Having undergone death and passed into the expanse of universal space it is as though in the physical world we were to meet a man and perceive only his thoughts without seeing the man himself. We should see a cloud of thoughts. After death we do not at first encounter beings; we encounter thoughts, the universal World-Intelligence.

In this sphere of cosmic Intelligence man lives for a few days after his death. And in the weaving cosmic thoughts there appears as it were a single cloud in which he sees the record of his last earthly life. This record is inscribed into the cosmic Intelligence. For a few days he beholds his whole

71

life in one great, simultaneous tableau. During these few days what is inscribed into the cosmic Intelligence becomes steadily fainter and fainter. The record expands into cosmic space and vanishes. Whereas at the end of earthly life the aspect of death appears, a few days after the end of this experience there comes the vanishing into cosmic space. Thus, after the first aspect, which we may call the aspect of death, we have the second aspect, which may be called the *aspect of the vanishing of earthly life*. After death there is actually for every human being a moment of terrible fear that he may lose himself, together with all his earthly life, in cosmic space.

If we wish for more understanding of man's experiences after death, Imaginative Knowledge will be found to be inadequate; we must pass on to the second stage of higher knowledge, to Inspiration. Imaginative Knowledge has pictures before it—pictures that are in the main like dream-pictures, except that we can never feel convinced of any reality behind the latter, whereas the pictures of Imagination, through their own inherent quality, always express reality. Through Imagination we live in a picture-world that is nevertheless reality. This picture-world must be transcended if we are to see what a man experiences after death when the few days during which he reviewed his life, have passed.

Inspiration, which must be acquired after or during the stage of Imagination, presents no pictures; instead of pictures there is spiritual *hearing*. Knowledge through Inspiration absorbs cosmic Intelligence, cosmic thoughts, in such a way that they seem to be spiritually heard. From all sides the cosmic word resounds, indicating distinctly that there is reality behind it. First comes the proclamation; then, when a man can give himself up to this Inspiration, he begins, in Intuition, to perceive behind the cosmic thoughts, the Beings of the Universe themselves. *Pictures* of the spiritual are perceived in Imagination; in Inspiration the spiritual *speaks;* Intuition perceives the *Beings themselves.* I said that the world is filled with cosmic thoughts. These in themselves do not at once point to beings; but we eventually become aware of words behind the thoughts and then of beholding through Intuition, the Beings of the Universe.

The first aspect of man's existence is the aspect of death—it is the earthly aspect; the second aspect leads us out into cosmic space, into which, as earthly men, we otherwise gaze without any understanding; this is the aspect of the vanishing of man's life. The third aspect presents the boundary of visible space: this is the *aspect of the stars*. But the stars do not appear as they do to physical sight. For physical sight the stars are points of radiance at the boundaries of the space in the direction towards which we are looking. If we have acquired the faculty of Intuitive Knowledge, the stars are the revealers of cosmic Beings, spiritual Beings. And with Intuition we behold in the spiritual Universe, instead of the physical stars, colonies of spiritual Beings at the places where we conceive the physical stars to be situated. The third aspect is the aspect of the stars. After we have learnt to know death, after we have recognised cosmic Intelligence through the widths of space, this third aspect leads us into the spheres of cosmic-spiritual Beings and thereby into the sphere of the stars. And just as the Earth has received man between birth and death, so, when he has crossed the abyss to cosmic Intelligence a few days after his death, he is received into the world of stars. On Earth he was a man of Earth among Earth-beings; after death he becomes a being of Heaven among heavenly Beings.

The first sphere into which man enters is the Moon-sphere; later on he passes into the other cosmic spheres. At the moment of death he still belongs to the Earth-sphere. But at that moment, everything within the range of earthly knowledge loses its significance. On the Earth there are different substances, different metals, and so on. At the moment of death all this differentiation ceases. All external solid substances are earthy; at the moment of death man is living in earth, water, air and warmth. In the sphere of cosmic Intelligence he sees his own life; he is between the region of Earth and the region of Heaven. A few days after death he enters the region of Heaven: first, the Moon-sphere.

In this Moon-sphere we meet cosmic Beings for the first time. But these cosmic Beings are still rather like human beings for at one time they were together with us on the Earth. In my books you can read how the physical Moon was once united with the Earth and then separated from it to form an independent cosmic body. It was, however, not the physical Moon alone that separated from the Earth. At one time there were among men on Earth great, primeval Teachers; it was they who brought the primordial wisdom to mankind. These great Teachers were not present on Earth in physical human bodies, but only in etheric bodies. When a man received instruction from them, he absorbed it inwardly. After a time, when the Moon separated from the Earth, these ancient Teachers went with it and formed a colony of Moon Beings. These primeval Teachers of mankind, long since separated from the Earth, are the first cosmic Beings to be encountered a few days after death.

The life spent with the Moon Beings during this period after death is related in a remarkable way to earthly existence. It might be imagined that man's life after death is more fleeting, less concrete, than earthly life. In a certain respect, however, this is not the case. If we are able to follow a man's experiences after death with supersensible vision we find that for a long time they have a much stronger effect upon him than anything in the earthly life which, in comparison, is like a dream. This period after death lasts for about a third of the time of life on Earth. What is now experienced differs with different individuals. When a man looks back over his earthly life he succumbs to illusion. He sees only the days and pays no heed to what he has experienced spiritually in sleep. Unless he is particularly addicted to sleep a man will, as a general rule, spend about a third part of his life in that state. After death he goes through it all in conscious connection with the Moon Beings. We live through these experiences because the great primeval Teachers of mankind pour the essence of their being into us, live in and with us; we live through the unconscious experiences of the nights on Earth as reality far greater than that of the earthly life.

Let me illustrate this by an example. Perhaps some of you know my Mystery Plays and will remember among the characters a certain Strader. Strader is a figure based upon a personality who is now dead but was alive when the first three Plays were written. It was not a matter of portraying his earthly life but the character was founded on the life of a man who was exceptionally interesting to me. Coming from comparatively simple circumstances, he first became a priest, then abandoned the Church and became a secular scholar with a certain rationalistic trend. The whole of this man's inner struggle interested me. I tried to understand it spiritually and wrote the Mystery Plays while watching his earthly life. After his death the interest I had taken in him enabled me to follow him during the period of existence he spent in the Moon-sphere. To-day (1924) he is still in that sphere. From the moment this individuality broke through to me with all the intense reality of the life after death, whatever interest I once had in his earthly life was completely extinguished. I was now living with this individuality after his death, and the effect upon me was that I could do no other than allow the character in the fourth Mystery Play to die, because he was no longer before me as an earthly man.— This is quoted merely in corroboration of the statement that experience of the life after death has far greater intensity, greater inner reality, than the earthly life; the latter is like a dream in comparison.

We must remember that after death man passes into the great Universe, into the Cosmos. He himself now becomes the Cosmos. He feels the Cosmos as his body, but he also feels that what was outside him during his earthly life is now *within* him. Take a simple example. Suppose you were once carried away by emotion during your earthly life and had struck someone a blow which caused him not only physical pain but also moral suffering. Under the influence of the Moon Beings after death you experience this incident differently. When you struck an angry blow, perhaps with a certain inner satisfaction, you did not feel the suffering of the man you struck. Now, in the Moon-sphere, you experience the physical pain and the suffering *he* had to endure. In the Moon-sphere you experience what you did or thought during your earthly life, not as you felt it, but as it affected the other person. After death, for a period corresponding to a third part of his lifetime, a man lives through, in backward order, everything that he thought and whatever wrong he did during his earthly life. It is revealed to him by the Moon Beings as intense reality. When I was inwardly accompanying Strader, for instance, in his life after death—he died in 1912 and is called Strader in the Mystery Plays although that was not his real name—he was experiencing first what he had experienced last in his earthly life, then the earlier happenings, and so on, in backward order. When he now comes before my soul he is living through in the Moon-sphere what he had experienced in the year 1875. Up to now he has been experiencing backwards the time between 1912 and 1875 and will continue in this way until the date of his birth.

This life after death in the sphere of the Moon Beings— who were once Earth Beings—is lived through for a third of the time of a man's life. The first seed of what is fulfilled as karma in the following earthly lives, arises here. In this life, which corresponds to a third part of his earthly lifetime, a man becomes inwardly aware, through his own feeling and perception, of how his deeds have affected others. And then a strong desire arises within him as spirit-man that what he is now experiencing in the Moon-sphere as the result of his dealings with other men on Earth may again be laid upon him, in order that compensation may be made. The resolve to fulfil his destiny in accordance with his earthly deeds and earthly thoughts comes as a wish at the end of the Moon-period. And if this wish—which arises from experience of the whole of the earthly life back to birth—is devoid of fear, the man is ready to be received into the next sphere, the Mercury-sphere, into which he then passes. In the Mercury-sphere he is instructed by the Beings whose realm he has entered—Beings who have never been on Earth, who were always supersensible Beings; in their realm he learns how to shape his further destiny. Thus, to learn what a man goes through between death and a new birth, corresponding in his spiritual existence to what he experienced among earthly beings between birth and death, we must follow him through the Mercury-sphere, the Venus-sphere and the Sun-sphere. For the totality of man's life consists in the earthly existence between birth and death and the heavenly existence between death and a new birth. This constitutes his life in its totality, and of this we will speak in the next lectures.

LECTURE 6

In the lecture yesterday I spoke of how man ascends after
death into the supersensible world and then lives through the
experiences connected with the first decades of his post-
mortem existence. I said that he spends a certain number of
years in the Moon-sphere, coming into contact there with
Beings who once lived on the Earth, not in physical but in
etheric bodies. These Beings were the Teachers of primeval
humanity, inspiring men with the profound wisdom that
once existed on Earth and gradually faded away. When the
physical Moon separated from the Earth, these Beings went
with it; their existence has continued on the Moon and man
encounters them there after his death when he is looking
back upon his earthly life and living through its experiences.

I have already said that when a man has lived long enough
in the Moon-region, he passes into the Mercury-region.
Here he encounters Beings who lead him into a part of the
Universe where the Beings are completely different from
those on Earth. To this region, however, man belongs
between death and a new birth just as surely as during his
earthly life he belonged to the Earth.

Let me now add something to the brief sketch given yesterday.—When a man passes through death—this actually takes
very little time—he begins his existence in the elements of
earth, water, fire and air. Substances that are differentiated
on Earth—metals and all other substances—are no longer
differentiated when death has actually taken place. All solid
substances are 'earth', all fluids are 'water', all gaseous
substances are 'air', and everything that radiates warmth is
'fire' (or 'warmth'). At the moment of death man is living
in this fourfold differentiation of substance. He passes then

79

into the region of cosmic Intelligence. Cosmic thoughts live and weave through this region in which he remains for a few days. Then he reaches the Moon-region which I have already described, and from there passes into the Mercury-region.

Let me repeat the sequence: man passes first into the region of the Elements, then into the region of cosmic Intelligence, then into the region of the Stars—first the Moon-region, then the Mercury-region.

We will now consider how a man's life in the Moon-region can have a determining effect upon his karma. Before his death he has pursued this or that course in his earthly life, has done good or evil. And with all this behind him he appears before the Moon Beings. These Moon Beings pronounce stern judgment, a cosmic verdict, upon the value or the reverse of good or bad actions for the Universe. A man must then leave behind him in the Moon-region the results of his evil actions, everything whereby he has done harm to the Universe. In so doing he leaves a part of himself behind. We must realise more strongly than is usual that man and his deeds and achievements form a unity, that his whole being is bound up with a good or with a bad deed. So that if we have to leave behind us the evil we have wrought, we have to leave part of ourselves behind. In point of fact we pass from this Moon-region with only the good we have achieved for the Universe and we are, therefore, mutilated in a certain sense, the extent or degree of mutilation depending upon how far we have allowed evil thoughts to become part of our own being. Everything by which we have injured the Cosmos must be left behind in the Moon-region.

If we wish to study man's further progress between death and a new birth, the following facts must be remembered. Man on the Earth is a being whose members are clearly distinguishable from each other. The head takes shape in the embryo and is the most highly developed member; the rest of man's bodily make-up was still unfinished during embryonic life. In a certain sense this remains the case through the whole of life. The head is the most highly elaborated part of man. After death, however, it is precisely the spiritual part of the head that passes away most rapidly in the spiritual world; it disappears almost entirely during the passage through the Moon-region. You must of course understand me correctly: the physical substance falls away with the corpse, but in the head there is not only physical substance, there are forces—supersensible forces—which form and imbue man's physical body with life. These forces pass through the gate of death and are recognised by Imaginative cognition as the spirit-form of man; the head of this spirit-form, however, is seen to be steadily disappearing. What actually remains, and can be mutilated, is the rest of the body apart from the head. If a man has in the main been a good man, this part of him can enter the Mercury-sphere more or less complete, whereas if he has been a bad character it will enter that sphere greatly mutilated. With these forces enveloping the soul we pass into our further life between death and a new birth, and it is from these forces that we have to build up the whole of our life during that period.

The spiritual Beings of the Mercury-sphere, who have never assumed human form and in whose environment we now find ourselves, have an important task. From the being who now appears as a headless man—if I may use the expression—all moral blemish has been removed in the Moon-sphere, but not the outcome of the health or illness undergone during earthly life. This is important, for it is both significant and surprising that although a man lays aside his moral blemishes in the Moon-region, the spiritual effects of whatever has befallen him in the shape of illness can only be removed in the Mercury-region, by those Beings who have never been men.

It is very important to pay attention to the fact that the spiritual consequences of illnesses are taken away from men in the Mercury-region. From this we realise that in the world of stars—which is actually the world of the Gods—the physical and the moral interweave. A moral blemish cannot enter the spiritual world; it remains behind in the Moon-region, the inhabitants of which are Beings especially concerned with men, because at one time they lived among them. The Beings indwelling Mercury were never inhabitants of the Earth. It is these Beings who take away from man the consequences of illnesses. The illnesses are seen streaming out as it were into cosmic space; their spiritual consequences are absorbed into the spiritual cosmos and the process is actually fraught with a kind of satisfaction. For the man who experiences this between death and a new birth it will be the first impression, a purely spiritual one, and yet as real to him as anything in earthly existence. Just as here on Earth we experience the wind, the lightning, the flow of water, so, when we have passed through the gate of death and entered the Mercury-region, do we experience the departure of the spiritual effects of illnesses. We see how they are absorbed by the spiritual Beings and we are left with the impression: Now be propitiated, O ye Gods!—I can only touch on this to-day; tomorrow we shall be able to go more deeply into this experience of how the Gods are pro-pitiated for the evil done on Earth—propitiated as a result of the effects of illnesses streaming out into the wide Universe.

These important facts of life between death and a new birth were once known to men, in the days when the Beings who afterwards became Moon-dwellers—the great primeval Teachers—were at hand to instruct them. Then, too, men recognised that the truth concerning the nature of illnesses can be known only when the truth comes from the Mercury Beings; hence all medical knowledge, all knowledge of heal-ing, was the secret of the Mercury Mysteries. In such Mysteries a man was not in the same position as he is in the universities of to-day. Higher Beings from the regions of the stars actually worked through the rites enacted in these Mysteries. In those ancient days the Gods themselves were men's teachers, and medicine was the wisdom transmitted to them directly by the Mercury Beings in the Mysteries; hence this ancient medicine was regarded by men as a gift of the Gods. Fundamentally speaking, whatever is effective in medicine to-day either originates from olden times, as an aftermath of what men learnt from the Mercury Gods, or it must be rediscovered through those methods which enable men eventually to have converse with the Gods, to learn from them. The stream of ancient wisdom has run dry, has disappeared; a new wisdom, based once again upon intercourse with the Gods, must be found. This is the mission of Anthroposophy in all the different domains.

From the Mercury-region man comes into the region of the Venus-existence. The Beings who inhabit Venus and are far more remote from earthly beings than the inhabitants of Mercury, will change what he brings with him into this region in such a way that it can advance to further stages in the spiritual world. This, however, is possible only because on passing into the Venus-region, man enters into a new element. While we are living here on Earth, much depends upon our having thoughts, concepts, ideas. For what would a man be on Earth without them? Thoughts are useful, and we as human beings are intelligent because we have thoughts that have some value. Especially at the present time it is very important that man should be intelligent. Nearly everyone is intelligent nowadays; it was not always so but to-day it certainly is. And after all, the whole of earthly life depends upon the fact that men have thoughts. The splendid achievements of technology have all sprung from human thoughts; everything good or bad that man brings about on Earth has sprung ultimately from his thoughts. And in the Moon-region thoughts are still an important factor, for the judgment of the Beings in that region is based upon how the good or bad deeds have arisen from thoughts. The Beings in the Mercury-region too, still judge the illnesses from which they must liberate men, according to the thoughts. But here, in a certain sense, is the boundary up to which thought—anything that recalls human intelligence—has significance, for the Venus-region into which man now passes, is ruled by what is known to us on Earth, in its reflection, as love. Here, love takes the place of wisdom; we enter the region of love. Man can pass into the Sun-existence only when love leads him into it out of the sphere of wisdom.

The following question may suggest itself to you: How does a man actually experience these things of which he becomes aware through spiritual perception?—You will no doubt have read what I have written about exercises for the soul in the book, *Knowledge of the Higher Worlds and its Attainment*, and will know that a man may gradually develop this perception through such exercises. When he succeeds in developing Imaginative consciousness he first experiences his whole life back to his birth, presented in one great spiritual tableau. What is experienced in a natural way after death is experienced through Initiation at any moment of life. When this experience reaches the stage of Inspiration, however, it reveals something that shines through this tableau of human life. Now this is the significant point: we cannot speak truly about the concatenation of the secrets underlying these things until we have reached a certain age. This has always been so. A man may be initiated at any time of life, but it is only at a certain age that through his own perception of these things he is able to have an all-embracing survey of cosmic secrets.

The reason is that when a man looks back over his life-tableau it presents itself in sections or phases of seven years: a first section from birth to approximately the seventh year, a second from the seventh to the fourteenth year, again from the fourteenth to the twenty-first year, then a section which includes the years from the twenty-first to the forty-second, then a section from the forty-second to the forty-ninth year, another from the forty-ninth to the fifty-sixth year and from the fifty-sixth to the sixty-third year. These sections of life are surveyed one after the other. In the first section of the retrospect, everything up to the change of teeth is seen simultaneously. The secrets of the Cosmos appear throughout as if seen through a mist. In the first section, from birth to the seventh year, the mysteries of the Moon are revealed as though the Sun were shining through a mist; the man is surveying them through his own etheric body. What I have told you to-day about his faults and ill-doings being left behind, and what I have told you about the Moon Beings—

84

all this stands written in the first section of this book of life.

Looking back over his life with Imagination, Inspiration and Intuition, it becomes clear to a man that this life has one, two, three, up to seven, chapters. In the first chapter, which comprises early childhood, are the Moon-mysteries. In the second chapter, comprising the period between the change of teeth and puberty, are the Mercury-mysteries. Doctors know well that this is the age when children's ailments are prevalent, but for all that it is the healthiest age in human life; taking into consideration mankind as a whole, the rate of mortality is relatively lowest in this period. The Mercury-mysteries are revealed behind this age of life, so that in the unlikely event of someone being initiated already at the age, say, of eighteen, he would be able to survey the Moon-mysteries and the Mercury-mysteries. If in later life a man looks back on the next section, from the fourteenth to the twenty-first year, everything in the Universe connected with the Venus-mysteries is revealed. In this period, when physical love arises in human life, the mysteries of the Venus-existence in the Universe are spiritually inscribed in the book of life. The period from the twenty-first to the forty-second year needs a survey three times more comprehensive than before, because here all the Beings of the Sun-mysteries are revealed. To be able to look back, we must be over the age of forty-two and then, in this section of life, we see in retrospect the Sun-mysteries. And when we are old enough to look back on the section of life from the forty-second to the forty-ninth year, the Mars-mysteries are revealed. But to penetrate the Mars-mysteries we must have passed the age of forty-nine. A man may be initiated, but to penetrate into the Mars-mysteries through his own power of vision, he must be able to look back upon the section of life between the forty-second and forty-ninth years. After the age of forty-nine he can look back upon the Jupiter-mysteries; and—I am myself now able to speak of this—after his sixty-third year he is allowed by decree of the Gods, to speak of the Saturn-mysteries too.

85

In this life between death and rebirth man passes farther and farther away from conditions surrounding him on Earth and enters into quite different ones. Having passed through the Venus-region, he experiences the realities of the Sun-sphere. And now, having described how these truths are revealed through Initiation, I can continue the study of man's existence between death and a new birth.

As we find our way into the spirit-world we are brought nearer and nearer to Beings of a higher rank than man. In the Moon-region we are still among Beings who, in the main, have lived with men on Earth, but here we already perceive those Beings who lead us on Earth from one life to another. These are the Beings I have called in my books—in accordance with ancient Christian usage—the Hierarchy of Angels. Looking back to early childhood with the Initiation-knowledge of which I have spoken, we see at the same time what has been wrought in man by the world of the Angels. Think of the wonderful beauty of some of the conceptions which exist in the simple hearts of men and are actually confirmed by the higher wisdom of Initiation. We speak of how the activities of the Angels weave through a child's first years of life; and when we look back in order to study the Moon-region we actually see our childhood and with it the weaving work of the Angels. Then, when stronger forces begin to operate in the human being, when he reaches the school age, we perceive the work of the Archangels. They are important for us when we are studying the Mercury-existence, for then we are in the world of the Archangels.—There follows the age of puberty and the period from approximately the fourteenth to the twenty-first year. The Venus-mysteries are now seen in retrospect, shining through the tableau of the course of life. At the same time we learn that the Hierarchy of the Archai, the Primal Forces, are the Beings specially associated with the Venus-existence. And here we realise a significant truth—again something that is particularly striking—namely, that the Beings associated with the Venus-existence after the age of puberty are those who, as Primal Forces, were concerned with the genesis of the world itself, and in their reflection are again active in the formation of physical man in the sequence of the generations. The relation between the Cosmos and human life is revealed in this way.

We gaze then into the mysteries of the Sun-existence. What is the nature of the Sun according to modern physicists? An incandescent globe of gas, where burning gases diffuse light and heat. For the eyes of spirit this is a thoroughly childish conception! The truth is that if the physicists could organise an expedition to the Sun, they would be astonished to find everything entirely different from what they imagined. There are no cosmic gases there; human beings would not be consumed by flames if they could travel to the Sun. But if they came into the Sun-region they would be torn asunder—destroyed in that way. What, then, is the Sun, in reality?

When you walk about a room there may be people in it, or chairs which you knock against. Here (*drawing on blackboard*) are objects, and between them is empty space through which you walk. In the area in which we are at present, certain portions of space are filled by chairs or by yourselves; other portions are empty. If I take the chairs away and you come in, you will find only an empty space. Empty space is far more prevalent in the Cosmos. Here on Earth we do not know what has to be known in the Cosmos. In the Cosmos, space can even be empty of itself, so that at some points there is no space. In soda-water there are little bubbles, less dense than the water; these you can see—it is the bubbles you see, not the water. In the same way, when you look out into space, you may see nothing; but where the Sun is, there is even less than space. Suppose that here is the empty space of the Universe, and that in this empty space there is nothing, not even space, so that if you went there you would be sucked up and disappear. There is nothing there at all, nothing physical, not even space. It is the site of all that is spiritual. This is the nature of the Sun-existence about which the physicists would be so astonished. Only at the edge of this empty space is there something that begins to be as the

87

physicists suppose. In the corona of the Sun there are incandescent gases, but within this empty space there is nothing physical, not even space! It is all purely spiritual. Within this sphere there are Beings of three ranks: Exusiai, Dynamis and Kyriotetes. Into this region we enter when we have passed through the Venus-existence during the further period between death and a new birth. Then, when we look back—only we must have been more than forty-two years old—we see the reflection, as it were, of the Sun-nature. The greater part of a man's life between death and a new birth is spent among the Exusiai, Dynamis and Kyriotetes.

Now when, during this period between death and a new birth, man actually penetrates into the Sun-region, there is no similarity whatever with anything to which we are accustomed in the physical, earthly world. In this latter world we may have good intentions; but there may be someone near us whose intentions are the very reverse. We try to perform good actions but are only to some extent successful; in the case of the other person, however, everything succeeds. Looking back over our life after years or decades have passed, we come all too easily to the conclusion that in the physical, earthly course of things, it is not the case that good intentions or good deeds also have good consequences. For instance, on Earth we see the good punished and the bad rewarded, for the good may be unfortunate and the bad fortunate. There seems to be no connection between moral life and physical actuality. On the other hand, everything physical has its necessary consequences; magnetic force must attract iron, for example. Physical relationships alone are realised on Earth in our life between birth and death. In the Sun-existence there are no such relationships; there are only *moral* relationships. Everything moral in that sphere has the power of coming to realisation in an appropriate way. Goodness produces phenomena which bring blessing to men, whereas evil brings the opposite. Here on Earth, moral relationship is only ideal, and can be established as ideal only in an external, inadequate way, inasmuch as jurisprudence sees to it that evil is punished. In the Sun-region, moral relationships become reality. In this region man's every good intention, however feeble the thought, begins to be reality—a reality perceived by the Exusiai, Dynamis and Kyriotetes. Man is regarded by the Beings of the Sun-region according to the goodness he has in him, according to the way he was able to think and feel and experience. I cannot, therefore, describe the Sun-region to you theoretically but only in a living way. It is not easy to give a definition of the effect of this or that goodness in the Sun-region; one can only try to make it clear to the listeners by saying: If, as man in the Earth-region you have had a good thought, in the Sun-region between death and a new birth you will have converse with Exusiai, Dynamis and Kyriotetes. You will be able to lead a spiritual life in community with these Beings. If, however, you have had evil thoughts, though you have left them behind you in the Moon-region, you will be a lonely soul, abandoned by Exusiai, Dynamis and Kyriotetes. Thus in the Sun-region it is through our community with these Beings that goodness becomes reality. If our thoughts have not been good, we do not understand their language; if we have accomplished nothing good we cannot appear before them. The effect of our goodness is all reality in the Sun-region.

This study will be continued in the lecture to-morrow.

LECTURE 7

Paris, 25th May, 1924

We have spoken about the life between death and a new birth and have realised that after death man is received into a super-earthly world which becomes manifest to us on Earth only through its signs or tokens—the stars; for the stars are tokens of another world, indications of spiritual worlds within our ken during our life between death and a new birth. We have heard, too, how man enters a Moon-sphere, a Mercury-sphere, a Venus-sphere, and yesterday we began to think about the Sun-sphere. At the same time I explained how, through Initiation-knowledge, the nature of these worlds can be understood.

When through the methods described in my books, the power to look into the spiritual world has been acquired, we are able to survey in retrospect the whole of our earthly life. It lies there, displayed in a vast tableau, and we survey it in periods of time, each of about seven years' duration. We see our early childhood until the change of teeth, and with it the mystery of the Moon-sphere is revealed. The mystery of the Mercury-sphere is revealed by the retrospective survey of the period between the change of teeth at about the seventh year, and puberty. The mystery of the Venus-sphere is revealed by the retrospective survey of the period from the fourteenth or fifteenth year to the beginning of the twenties. And when, having grown older in earthly life, we look back on the period between approximately the twenty-first to the forty-second years—when the human being is in the prime of life and has not begun to decline—then the mysteries of the Sun-sphere present themselves to us. In this sphere there are no processes, no workings, of nature. None of the causes and effects to be perceived in earthly nature exist in the Sun-sphere. When we have passed the spheres of Moon, Mercury and Venus and have entered that of the Sun there are no activities of nature around us but only activities of a moral kind. Everything that is good has its corresponding good results; whatever is evil has long ago fallen away in the Moon-sphere. The Sun-sphere is pure goodness, shining, radiant goodness; no evil has any place in it. And we must live through this Sun-existence often for centuries, for time is more prolonged in the life between death and rebirth than here on Earth. In the Sun-sphere we come not only into the company of those souls with whom we were connected by karma on Earth, who have passed through the gate of death and have entered the spiritual world as we ourselves have done, but in the Sun-sphere we come also into the province of the Exusiai, Dynamis and Kyriotetes. The activities of these Beings are purely spiritual; their nature is purely spiritual. And the moral world we behold around us in the Sun-sphere belongs to them, just as the mineral, plant and animal kingdoms belong to the Earth.

To understand the life of the human soul in the Sun-sphere we must realise that here on Earth we stand spatially enclosed within our skin. We look out upon the world from what is bounded by our skin. In the Sun-sphere the reverse is the case. There, everything we here call the world is within us; the Moon is within us, not outside us; Mercury is within us; indeed the Sun-sphere itself is within us, not outside us.

Here in earthly life we distinguish between our body and our head, realising that if the head is to do its work as an organ of cognition it must be set apart from the rest of the body. And just as we know that the head must be constructed differently from the rest of the body, so, in the Sun-sphere we know that the world-organism is in us, belongs to us as Moon, Mercury, Venus, Sun. But we also have something special which corresponds to the head in earthly life, namely, Mars, Jupiter and Saturn. They constitute our head in the Sun-existence. We may say: In the Sun-existence, Moon, Mercury and Venus are our limbs; the Sun itself is our whole rhythmic system; the Sun-sphere itself, with all its Beings,

92

is our heart and our lungs; whereas our organ of intelligence and reason, the head, is represented in the Sun-sphere by Mars, Jupiter and Saturn. And just as we speak with the mouth in the lower part of the head, so, because we carry Mars within us in our cosmic body, we live by virtue of the cosmic word. The cosmic word sounds through the wide expanses of space. Thus, just as here on Earth we carry in our head those insignificant earthly thoughts, so through Jupiter we bear within us the wisdom of worlds. And as here we have memory, experiences of remembrance, so in the Sun-existence we bear within us the Saturn-existence which gives us cosmic memory. And just as here we live inside our skin and look outwards, so we live, as I have described, in our Sun-existence and look out upon the outside world, upon Man—not, of course, the being with whom anatomy is concerned, but a being as great, mighty and majestic as the Universe with all its stars.

Seen from an earthly standpoint we have far too low an opinion of what is comprised in man—and this is a good thing for earthly human beings who might otherwise become megalomaniacs. Fundamentally speaking, if we include all the human beings on the Earth, they are the bearers of all the Hierarchies, for the Beings of the Hierarchies unfold their nature in man. That in man which is far grander than the whole starry world, than the courses and phenomena of the stars—that is our outer world in the Sun-existence. And it is together with the Exusiai, Dynamis and Kyriotetes, with the other Beings belonging to the Moon-sphere, with the Angels, with the Beings who inhabit Venus, with the Hierarchy of the Archai, with all the other human souls with whom we are karmically connected, that we prepare our next earthly life. This work in the Sun-existence for the elaboration of the next earthly life is infinitely grander than anything man can achieve for culture and civilisation on the Earth. What earthly civilisation offers is, after all, the work of man. But man himself is much more; to him it is vouchsafed to work for his later earthly life in collaboration with the Beings in the Sun-sphere. The result would be pitiable if man were merely to work with other human souls at the structure subsequently produced for earthly life. He must work in co-operation with all the higher Hierarchies. For the being born of a mother has not arisen on the Earth; it is only the scene of action, as it were, that comes into existence on the Earth. A wonderful cosmic creation, formed in supersensible worlds, in the Sun-existence, incarnates into what is produced through physical heredity.

If such things are grasped with the right kind of understanding, we must surely look up to the Sun and say that its physical rays shining down to the Earth as warmth are the blessings bestowed by the Sun. But when we know what the Sun is in reality, we shall feel: Up yonder, where the glowing orb of the Sun moves through the Universe, is the scene where the spiritual prototypes of future generations of men first take shape; there the higher Hierarchies work together with the souls of men who lived on Earth in their previous incarnations, to bring the human beings of the future into existence. The Sun is actually the spiritual embryo of the Earth-life of the future. In point of fact, it is the first half of the Sun-existence that we spend with the Gods, shaping together with them our future Earth-existence.

When we have lived through half the period between death and a new birth and have reached the point called in my Mystery Plays, the 'Midnight Hour', another kind of work begins. We have heard that the Sun-existence is pure goodness. If all that I have described to you had been the work of the higher cosmic wisdom alone, angel-like, godlike beings would have come to the Earth instead of men. But these godlike beings would have had no freedom, for in keeping with the Sun-existence from which they sprang they would have been adapted only to do good. They would have had no choice between good and evil.

In the second half of the Sun-existence, part of the human reality produced there is transformed, dissolved as it were, to a picture. To begin with, man is formed in such a way that in his organism he would inevitably have become a wholly good being. Then, however, in the second half of the Sun-existence, part of his nature is not formed as a reality, but only as a picture, so that we go on our way in the Sun-sphere partly as spiritual reality, partly as a picture. This spiritual reality is the foundation for our body in the next earthly life. The part that is merely a picture is the foundation for our head. Because it is merely a picture it can be filled with much denser material, bony substance in fact. At the same time there is membered into this part that is not spiritual reality but a picture only, what we experience on Earth as the echoings of this picture. The requirements of our stomach, liver, and so on, are experienced as necessities of nature. The moral impulse within us is a spiritual experience here on Earth. The rudiment of what resounds from our conscience as the moral impulse is formed in that part of the Sun's embryonic prototype of man which becomes a picture.

Now the Earth in its evolution, the evolution of mankind on the Earth—each has its history; culture and civilisation evolve throughout the course of this history. The Sun-life, the long period traversed between death and a new birth, has also its history. The most important event in the Earth's history is the Mystery of Golgotha, and in that history we make a clear distinction between the period before the Mystery of Golgotha and the period after it. A similar distinction must be made in the Sun-existence between what took place there before the Event of Golgotha on Earth, and after it. The following are the facts.—

Before the Mystery of Golgotha had taken place the Christ Being was not present on the Earth; His coming was expected but He was not yet there, He was still in His Sun-existence. Those who were initiated in the Mysteries had ways and means in their Mystery Centres of participating in the Sun-life. When the Initiates succeeded in attaining higher knowledge outside the body, they were able, through their Initiation, to reach Christ in the Sun-sphere where He was to be found. Since the Mystery of Golgotha came to pass on the Earth, Christ has no longer been in the Sun-sphere. He has united Himself with Earth-existence. First, Christ is present in the Sun-sphere; afterwards He is no longer there. In Earth-life it is exactly the reverse: to begin with, Christ is not there; after the Mystery of Golgotha He *is*. But just as the Christ Impulse penetrates radically into Earth-life, so does it into the Sun-life. Here on Earth it costs us effort so to deepen our life of soul that we may experience the Christ, that we may be inwardly filled, permeated by the Christ; similarly, it is difficult during the Sun-life to survey, to behold, the essential nature of the whole man. And especially was it difficult in the early days of man's evolution, in spite of the instinctive clairvoyance then prevailing, to perceive the human being in the Sun-life after death. Precisely because on Earth man saw something spiritual within himself, it was difficult for him in the Sun-life to perceive the mystery of man as a world outside himself. Before the Mystery of Golgotha it was the Christ who gave to man in the Sun-sphere the power to behold his *whole* being. Since the Mystery of Golgotha we, as men on the Earth, must bring about the spiritual deepening that can be acquired through living contemplation of the Mystery of Golgotha, through inward participation in the life of Christ. In this way, during our earthly existence, we can consciously marshal the forces which we can bear with us through death and which can give us power to see man's whole being in the Sun-sphere. Before the Mystery of Golgotha, Christ gave to human beings in their life between death and rebirth the power to behold man in the Sun-existence; since the Mystery of Golgotha Christ prepares human beings during earthly life itself to be able to behold the whole, full nature of man in the Sun-existence. Thus it is only when we look out beyond Earth-existence into the Sun-existence that we can learn truly to understand the essence of Christianity. And, as we have seen, we learn to recognise in the Sun-existence a first half when man is originally formed as reality, when he is pure goodness. Then the picture-like part is engendered, and this projects into the later life, giving man freedom and containing the seed of *moral* experience.

Now if we study a man's moral aptitudes and the health-promoting forces in him with Initiation-science, we see nothing correctly through Imagination, Inspiration and Intuition unless these faculties are strengthened by what we can receive from the spheres into which man gradually enters on passing out of the Sun-existence—the spheres of Mars-existence, Jupiter-existence, Saturn-existence. Then, in order to fathom this second half of human life between death and rebirth, we must look back once more on certain seven-year periods in life. To see all this connectedly, however, we must have passed our sixty-third year, as I have already pointed out. If we look back on the period between the forty-second and forty-ninth years, the mysteries of Mars shine out from this period of life. From the forty-ninth to the fifty-sixth year, the Jupiter-mysteries send out their light, and from the period between the fifty-sixth and the sixty-third years of life, illumination comes from the Saturn-mysteries. Merely through the light which radiates towards us in this retrospective survey, we can understand what takes place in the spheres of Mars, Jupiter and Saturn to prepare man for a new life on Earth. For when a man enters these spheres, having passed through the Sun-existence, the Beings of the higher Hierarchies begin to work manifestly: first the Thrones in the Mars-sphere; then the Cherubim in the Jupiter-sphere; and the Seraphim in the Saturn-sphere.

When we have passed through this second half of the life between death and a new birth, once again the position is in a certain respect the opposite of that in earthly life. Here on Earth we look out into the wide spaces of the starry world, we see its wonders and its sublimity fills us with reverence. When in preparation for our future earthly life we proceed from the Sun-existence through the spheres of Mars, Jupiter and Saturn, wherever we look we are in the sphere of religious life. But looking downwards towards the Earth, it does not appear to us in a physical form as we have it around us here; rather there appears in the direction of the Earth a sublime and mighty spiritual life, woven out of the events of Mars, Jupiter and Saturn, out of the deeds of the Seraphim, Cherubim and Thrones. Now, however, it is not quite as it

97

was before, when we felt the whole world within us. We felt the Exusiai, Dynamis and Kyriotetes within ourselves. Now, looking down as we experience the deeds of Seraphim, Cherubim and Thrones, we see them, to begin with, outside ourselves; we see below us the supersensible heaven, for the purely spiritual world is, for us, even above that. We see the supersensible heaven and look down into the spheres of Mars, Jupiter, Saturn; we see Thrones, Cherubim and Seraphim living, striving, working. But what vista presents itself to us when we contemplate this work?—As we watch, we experience in a supersensible way among the Seraphim, Cherubim and Thrones what will constitute the fulfilment of our karma in the next earthly life; we see what we shall experience through those other men with whom our karma is in some way interwoven. This we experience in the first place through divine deeds among the Seraphim, Cherubim and Thrones. They determine among themselves what we shall experience as the fulfilment of our karma in the next life on Earth. The Gods are verily our creators, but they also create our karma. The fulfilment of our karma is first experienced by the Gods in a heavenly picture; and this makes the impression we carry with us into our further existence. We take our karma upon ourselves because we behold it first in the divine deeds of the Seraphim, Cherubim and Thrones. And in this vista we are shown what is in store for us in the next earthly life, carried into effect by the Gods.

From this you will realise that knowledge of karma is acquired through Initiation-science if human life is followed through the second half of the journey from death to a new birth and if we are able to decipher what takes place in the spheres of Mars, Jupiter and Saturn through the deeds of the Thrones, Cherubim and Seraphim. And for one who has learnt to look back in spirit over his life between his forty-second and forty-ninth years, it is possible to penetrate into the Mars-mysteries, to have some vision of what takes place in that sphere—especially among the Thrones but in general among Thrones, Cherubim and Seraphim—when man is passing through it. From the standpoint of earthly life alone, the way in which a man's karma works cannot be rightly judged; the supersensible world must come to our assistance. And if someone wishes to study karma, he must turn his attention to that part of the Universe traversed by man between death and a new birth in the spheres of Mars, Jupiter and Saturn. Now in certain cases what is taking place in the Mars-sphere is of particular significance for the next earthly life.

Between death and a new birth we look at the Mars-sphere and perceive what is happening there. Everything is 'word'. The Beings of Mars are 'word-beings'—if I may put it so. Picture it as follows. Man consists of flesh and blood; when he speaks he sets the air in motion. When the air-waves strike against our ears, we hear; the sounds and tones are embodied in the air-waves. The Mars Beings are formed of such waves; their whole nature consists of words, and when we hear with the ears of spirit we experience these Beings. If in later life we look back over the period between the forty-second and forty-ninth years, if this is the period that has the greatest influence on a man between death and a new birth, if it is in the Mars-sphere that his karma is chiefly worked out, then what he will experience on the Earth is very closely connected with the Mars-existence. At the decisive juncture in his life after death he looks down through the Mars-sphere and forms for himself an earthly life very strongly connected with the Mars-existence.

Now let us take an example. There was a man who lived at the time when the Arabs, under the influence of Mohammedanism, streamed from Asia and North Africa to battle against Europe, threatening the Spanish Empire and setting up Moorish-Arabian sovereignty. Suppose that before the spread of Arabian domination in Africa a man had acquired learning in the form customary at that time. There was such a man. In North Africa he had imbibed the knowledge that was available there, not exactly as it had been imbibed by St. Augustine, but in a somewhat similar form. This man—I am not now speaking of St. Augustine but of the other personality—imbibed a later form of North African learning

99

which by then contained elements of Moorish-Arabian thought. This personality subsequently went over to Spain where his beliefs underwent a kind of transformation; he turned to a more Christian point of view and mingled the Arabian concepts he had previously imbibed with the Christian teachings he was now receiving. Then he became imbued with elements of cabbalistic knowledge—not with what is now generally called Cabbalism but with certain trends of cabbalistic thought. The outcome was that he had many doubts, inner doubts and uncertainties; and in this mood of uncertainty he died. Comparatively soon afterwards, in the first half of the Middle Ages, this male personality was reborn as a woman, bringing into the new life an accumulation of all these doubts, which now became more deeply rooted than ever. The same personality appears again later on, having prepared for the transition from life as a woman to life again as a man, partly before and partly during the life between death and rebirth. The destiny for the next earthly life having been elaborated principally in the Mars-sphere, this personality was inevitably associated with the sphere of keen intellectuality on Earth—the sphere of intellectual judgments fraught with elements of criticism, of rebellion. This personality, two of whose previous incarnations I have here described, then became *Voltaire.*

You see how in the life between death and a new birth the earthly life is formed through the connection existing between man and the spiritual realities behind the stars. We understand the historical course of earthly life only when we can perceive the connection between one life and other earthly lives of the same individual.

How, then, do things that were present as causes and effects in earlier epochs of historical evolution pass over into the new epoch? It is men themselves who carry them over. All of you sitting here have brought over from your experiences in earlier epochs what you are experiencing in the present era. It is men themselves who make history, but we understand history only if instead of abstract speculation we are able to perceive what happens to individuals between death and a new birth in concrete reality.

Of particular importance for the understanding of human earthly life is the study of the karmic evolution that is revealed when a man brings with him from his earlier lives on Earth the results of having elaborated the main impulses of his karma in the Saturn-sphere. Men whose main karmic impulses take shape in the Mars-existence become like Voltaire. All their thoughts are concerned with life on Earth, criticising it, fighting against it, sometimes—in Voltaire's case with genius—epitomising it in caustic, aphoristic sayings. It is different when the karma is formed mainly through the Saturn-impulses. These Saturn-impulses have a very special influence on men. Even the perception of them when a man looks back upon his earthly life between the fifty-sixth and sixty-third years—even the sight of the Saturn-mysteries is in many respects shattering; these mysteries are in a sense alien to earthly life. And whoever gradually learns through Initiation-knowledge to perceive the Saturn-mysteries that are connected with this period of life, undergoes experiences of dramatic intensity, shattering experiences, that are harder and harder to bear because these mysteries strike at the very roots of life. Nevertheless it can be said that we become aware of the whole wonderful setting of the settings of a man's life when we perceive how karma takes shape in this sphere. I will illustrate this too by an example, but something must be said in preparation.

A question may well occur to you—a question that is entirely justified and based upon statements often made by me in books and lectures, namely, that in earlier times there were great Initiates who lived among men. You may ask: Where are they now, in this later age? Probably if you look around at present you will not say of many of the men working in the world that they have the characteristic traits of Initiates—and this has been the case for some long time. So the question must be asked: Where are the Initiates in their later incarnations?

Now someone who was an Initiate in a former incarnation,

in full consciousness and outwardly too, need not necessarily become one again in a subsequent incarnation. The fruits of the Initiation may remain in the subconsciousness. A man is obliged to make use of the body with which his epoch can provide him. The bodies of to-day are not well adapted for spiritual knowledge; they are actually a continual hindrance because they are products of a materialistic epoch; and the education we receive from childhood onwards is a greater hindrance still. When a person who was an Initiate in past ages grows up in these conditions, he cannot again give outward expression to what remained of the Initiation for this incarnation. We learn to write in childhood but our present writing is incapable of giving expression to what at one time was Initiation-science; and it is the same in other domains. Initiates of earlier epochs may appear in life as great figures in a different sense, but not as Initiates. Many a life at the present time and in the immediate past points back to earlier Initiation.

I should like to give you an example of a personality who in a former earthly life was actually initiated into a high grade of the Hibernian Mysteries, the Mysteries of ancient Ireland, during the first Christian century when those great Mysteries were already in decline, though still preserving far-reaching, profound knowledge. The knowledge possessed by these Irish Mysteries was especially profound, not in an intellectual but in an intensely human sense. An impression of the proceedings in these Mysteries can be described as follows: After a candidate had been prepared for a long time to realise that truth may be subject to deception on the Earth, to realise the possibility of doubt, he had to experience in a picture something that only in that form could make the necessary deep impression. The pupil was taken in front of two statues. One was made of elastic substance, but it was hollow. It was of huge dimensions and tremendously impressive. The pupil was told to touch it. This caused a violent shock, for the statue gave the impression of being alive. The finger was pressed into it, then quickly withdrawn, and the original shape was immediately restored.

The impression was of something living that was at once restored when disturbed even in the slightest degree. This was intended to signify everything in man that is of the nature of the Sun.

The other statue was more plastic. Again the pupil was told to touch it, and in this case the impression left by the touch, remained. The next day, however, when the pupil was led before the statue again, its original shape had been restored during the night. Ritualistic acts of this kind brought about a change in the inner life of the pupil of the Mysteries.

In this way a deep impression had been made in the Irish Mysteries upon a certain personality who was living at that time as a man. You will realise that when examples of this kind are being given to-day, the male incarnations are the most likely to be conspicuous because in earlier epochs it was almost exclusively men who played any important part. Incarnations as women are intermediate. To-day, when women are beginning to be important figures in historical life and development, the time is coming when female incarnations will be increasingly significant.

Now there is a personality upon whom the Initiation rites and ceremonies of the Hibernian Mysteries had made a profound impression; they had a deep effect upon his inner life and his experiences were of such intensity that he forgot the Earth altogether. Then, after this personality had lived through an incarnation as a woman, when the impulses of earlier Initiation showed themselves merely in the general disposition of the soul, he came to the Earth again as an important figure in the 19th century. He had lived out the consequences of his karma in the Saturn-sphere—the sphere where one lives among Beings who, fundamentally speaking, have no *present*. It is a shattering experience to look with clairvoyant vision into the Saturn-sphere, where Beings live who have no present but only look back on their past. Whatever they do is done unconsciously; any action of theirs comes to consciousness only when it has happened and is inscribed into the world-karma. Acquaintance with these

103

Beings who draw their past after them like a spiritual comet's tail, has a shattering effect. The personality of whom I am speaking, who had at one time been initiated and had thus transcended earthly existence in a certain sense, bore his soul to these Beings who take no part in the present, and elaborated his karma among them. It was as if everything that had been experienced hitherto in an Initiate-existence now illumined with majestic splendour all the past earthly lives. This past was brought to fruition by what had been experienced through the Hibernian Initiation. When this personality appeared again on Earth in the 19th century he had now, by contrast, to unfold impulses for the *future*. And when, on descending from the Saturn-sphere, this soul, with its gaze into the past illumined by the light of Initiation, arrived on Earth, it presented this contrast: a firm foothold on the Earth while gazing into the future and giving expression to far-reaching ideas, impulses and perceptions. This Hibernian Initiate became *Victor Hugo*. We can assess a man rightly only when we also perceive the development he underwent between death and a new birth. His moral, religious and ethical qualities then become evident to us. A personality certainly does not become poorer but on the contrary, very much richer, when viewed with the eyes of spirit.

These examples have been selected with the greatest exactitude. How do they help us to understand the life of man, the collaboration of the Cosmos with man? How does a third example help us to understand much that might otherwise be problematical even to unprejudiced minds? How do the karmic connections in such a case explain something quite extraordinary, something which otherwise seems incomprehensible?

We are led to Mysteries that had fallen completely into decay. These Mysteries had at one time been a factor of great significance in America but had then become decadent, with the result that conceptions of the rites, and their actual enactment, had become thoroughly childish in comparison with the grandeur of earlier times. But even the elements of superstition and magic prevailing in these later Mysteries before the so-called 'discovery' of America—therefore not so very long ago—still echoed something of the suggestive power of the most ancient Mysteries.

There was a personality who received in these later Mysteries not only pictures but definite impressions of Beings then known by the names of Taotl, Quetzalcoatl, Tezcalipoca. These Beings made a tremendously strong impression, but it was an impure influence—impure in an ethical respect, as is often the case with decadent Mysteries. I see this personality born again later on as a man whose subconsciousness was permeated with the suggestive power that emanated from these Mysteries. He was reborn as *Éliphas Lévi* and his writings revive the abstract, rationalistic, purely external conceptions which invariably spring from decadent Mysteries. This throws light on an otherwise enigmatic figure, whose writings have a certain grandeur about them but also something that is apt to stupefy the soul.

No matter where we look, life is clarified by the concrete indications given by Anthroposophy. Is it now possible for you to suppose that genuine descriptions of conditions of existence above and beyond earthly life can be listened to without stirrings of the heart, without spiritual warmth and illumination being brought into your souls? Does not human life between birth and death look different, indeed is it not felt to be different, when these descriptions of supersensible life are allowed to work upon the soul with all their inner power? We realise that we have come down from a world that can indeed be described; we carry into the physical world something that has lived among Gods.

To grasp these things theoretically is of very secondary importance. What matters is to realise that as human beings on the Earth in the physical body it is incumbent upon us to become worthy of what we have brought with us from supersensible worlds. If knowledge becomes an impulse of will worthy of our soul-life before the descent through birth, then what is taught in Anthroposophy has a direct moral influence. This strengthening of the moral impulse is an essential aspect of Anthroposophy. I think the content of these three lectures will have made this evident.

Let us now look at the other aspect, the aspect of death which ends physical life on Earth, setting Nothingness in the place of life. If, however, we can picture what it has been possible to describe of the supersensible world, then behind the Nothingness there rises the spiritual world of the Gods, and man becomes conscious that he will have the strength to begin the work of forming a new physical body just where the Nothingness of his former physical body has been made evident. This gives a strong and true religious impulse. And so a picture of cosmic and human life springs from Anthroposophy. Anthroposophy is moreover the source from which moral and religious ideals are imbued with strength.

I should like to conclude these lectures by speaking of the living Anthroposophy that must remain with us, so that even when we separate in space we are together in spirit. Our thoughts will meet and in reality we are not parting at all. Through study of supersensible realities we know that those who have been brought together by Anthroposophy can always be together in soul and in spirit. Therefore let these lectures to the Group here conclude on this note: You and I have been together for a time in space, and in spirit we will remain united.

———

Introductory Address.

My dear friends:

The last time I was able to speak to at least a few of you, the first Goetheanum in Dornach was still in existence. It was a great pleasure for me then to address a number of friends from France and this pleasure is repeated now, when I have been invited to speak here too about matters of fundamental interest to Anthroposophy. I thank those friends, especially Mademoiselle Sauerwein, for their kind invitation, and I am also grateful to Dr. Jules Sauerwein who translated the lectures in Dornach so very ably, for undertaking to do this in Paris too.

Certain changes have come about in the Anthroposophical Movement, through the fact that comparatively soon after the misfortune of the fire, we were able to hold the Christmas Meeting which has, I believe, given a new impulse to the Anthroposophical Movement—above all to the content of anthroposophical activity. The new feature in the Movement is that I myself have been obliged to take over the Presidency, whereas hitherto I merely regarded myself as a teacher. The decision I had to make was a very critical one, even in relation to the spiritual world. It was a venture, because my assumption of the external leadership of the Society might have meant fewer revelations from spiritual Beings—and such revelations are obviously essential to the spread of Anthroposophy.

But to-day I am able to recognise the extremely significant fact that since the Christmas Meeting the impulse which must come down from the spiritual worlds if the Anthroposophical Movement is to make real progress, has grown even stronger. Consequently, since the Christmas Meeting our Movement has become, and will continue to become, more and more esoteric in the true sense of the word. Connected with this, however, it must be realised that very strong hostile powers, demonic powers, are battling against the Movement. It is to be hoped, nevertheless, that the forces behind the alliance we were able to establish at the Christmas Meeting with the good spiritual Powers will be able in future times to quell all those hostile Powers in spiritual realms which make use of human beings on Earth to attain their ends.

NOTES

PAGE
15 *Garibaldi*, 1807–1882. The maiden name of his Brazilian wife was Anita Riveira de Silva.
23 '*Negative space*'. See *Physical and Ethereal Spaces*, by George Adams; also *Plant, Sun, Earth*, by George Adams and Olive Whicher.
46 *Haroun al Raschid*, 764–809.
47 *Ernst Haeckel*, 1834–1919.
47 *Gregory VII*, Pope from 1053 to 1085.
49 *Bacon of Verulam*, 1561–1626.
50 *Amos Comenius*, 1592–1671.
57 *geometry teacher*, see *The Course of my Life* (Rudolf Steiner's autobiography), chapter II.
58 *Lord Byron*, 1788–1824.
60 *Carl Marx*, 1818–1883.
60 *Helsingfors lecture-course:* 'The Occult Foundations of the Bhagavad Gita'. 9 lectures, May/June, 1913.
60 *Muawiyah*, Caliph in Syria from 661 to 680. Founded the dynasty of the Omayyads.
65 *Maurice Maeterlinck on Rudolf Steiner*. See *Le Grand Secret*, p. 253 (Bibliothèque Charpentier, Paris, 1921). The words referred to are as follows:
'Steiner . . . nous décrit les transformations successives des entités qui deviendront des hommes, et il le fait avec tant d'assurance qu'on se demande, après l'avoir suivi avec intérêt à travers des préliminaires qui dénotent un esprit très pondéré, très logique et très vaste, s'il devient subitement fou ou si l'on a affaire à un mystificateur ou à un véritable voyant. . . ."
100 *Voltaire*, 1694–1778.
104 *Victor Hugo*, 1802–1885.
105 *Éliphas Lévi* (Alphonse Louis Constant), 1810–1875. His principal works are: *Doctrine and Ritual of Transcendental Magic* and *The History of Magic*. Both translated into English by A. E. Waite.

Longer references to the individuals named above will be found in Vols. I–IV of *Karmic Relationships: Esoteric Studies*. See the Summary of Contents in each case.

Publisher's Note Regarding Rudolf Steiner's Lectures

The lectures contained in this volume have been translated from the German which is based on stenographic and other recorded texts that were in most cases never seen or revised by the lecturer. Hence, due to human errors in hearing and transcription, they may contain mistakes and faulty passages. Every effort has been made to ensure that this is not the case. Some of the lectures were given to audiences more familiar with anthroposophy; these are the so-called 'private' or 'members' lectures. Other lectures, like the written works, were intended for the general public. The differences between these, as Rudolf Steiner indicates in his *Autobiography*, is twofold. On the one hand, the members' lectures take for granted a background in and commitment to anthroposophy; in the public lectures this was not the case. At the same time, the members' lectures address the concerns and dilemmas of the members, while the public work speaks directly out of Steiner's own understanding of universal needs. Nevertheless, as Rudolf Steiner stresses: 'Nothing was ever said that was not solely the result of my direct experience of the growing content of anthroposophy. There was never any question of concessions to the prejudices and preferences of the members. Whoever reads these privately printed lectures can take them to represent anthroposophy in the fullest sense. Thus it was possible without hesitation—when the complaints in this direction became too persistent—to depart from the custom of circulating this material "for members only". But it must be borne in mind that faulty passages do occur in these reports not revised by myself.' Earlier in the same chapter, he states: 'Had I been able to correct them [the private lectures] the restriction [for members only] would have been unnecessary from the beginning.'